GEOMETRIC TREND
Copyright © 2017 Instituto Monsa de ediciones

Editor, concept, and project director
Anna Minguet

Co-autor
Carolina Amell

Project's selection, design and layout
Carolina Amell (Monsa Publications)
Cover design
Carolina Amell (Monsa Publications)

INSTITUTO MONSA DE EDICIONES
Gravina 43 (08930)
Sant Adrià de Besòs
Barcelona (Spain)
Tlf. +34 93 381 00 50
www.monsa.com
monsa@monsa.com

Visit our official online store!
www.monsashop.com

ISBN: 978-84-16500-42-0
D.L. B 1398-2017
Printed by Impuls45

GEOMETRIC TREND

BY CAROLINA AMELL

91.

it is
what
it is

N°10

Linus Lohoff
Art Direction &
Photography

57.

165.

169.

Intro

Geometry imposes on the design. It not only manifests itself in clothing; Dresses, skirts, shorts, pants and blazers, but also accessories such as rings, necklaces, handbags, tattoo, furniture... The concept is to use simple lines, embellishing in a minimalist way, these are the characteristics that best define this tendency, no matter the shape, color or mixture of combinations.

In this book you will see how different design studies, combine geometry on surfaces, to decorate the interior of the home, the skin, or use as a corporate image of a company.

La geometría se impone en el diseño. No sólo ha decidido manifestarse en prendas de ropa; vestidos, faldas, shorts, pantalones y blazers, sino también en accesorios como anillos, collares, bolsos, tattoo, muebles... El concepto es usar líneas sencillas, que embellecen de forma minimalista, esas son las características que mejor definen esta tendencia, no importa la forma, el color o la mezcla de combinaciones entre las figuras.

A continuación veréis como diferentes estudios de diseño, combinan la geometría en superficies, para decorar el interior del hogar, la piel, o usar como imagen corporativa de una empresa.

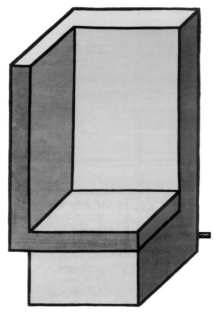

11.

67.

London

02.

COUNTRY
UNITED KINGDOM
POPULATION
8,416,535
COORDINATES
51°30' 26"N
0°7' 39"W

COLOURS

WWW.RICHBARCLAYDESIGNS

19.

43.

75.

Index

cc-tapis

www.cc-tapis.com

Photo by Lorenzo Gironi, styling by MOtel409 and Studiomilo

All cc-tapis® rugs are completely handknotted by expert Tibetan artisans in Nepal. cc-tapis utilises only hand-spun materials including himayalan wool, pure silk and hand-carded aloe. No chemicals, acids or artificial fibres are ever used in our process. A strong respect for the materials & for the culture of this ancient craft is reflected in cc-tapis eco-friendly approach.

cc-tapis has 6 collections, each of them experiment and interpret aesthetics and knotting techniques in their own unique way.

Todas las alfombras de cc-tapis® son confeccionadas exclusivamente a mano por expertos artesanos tibetanos de Nepal. cc-tapis utiliza sólo materiales hilados a mano, entre ellos lana del Himalaya, seda pura y aloe cardado a mano. En nuestro proceso no se utilizan en ningún momento productos químicos, ácidos o fibras artificiales. El enfoque de cc-tapis, respetuoso con el medio ambiente, refleja su enorme consideración por los materiales y la cultura de este ancestral oficio.

cc-tapis cuenta con 6 colecciones, en cada una de las cuales se experimentan e interpretan la estética y técnicas de tejido de un modo exclusivo.

Visioni's rug collection (left page)

VISIONI_Patricia Urquiola

Project Name: Visioni

Client: cc-tapis
Visioni, the new rugs by Patricia Urquiola for cc-tapis. An unprecedented synthesis between an age-old technique and contemporary graphics. Patricia Urquiola was born in Oviedo (Spain) in 1961. She lives and works in Milan.

Visioni, las nuevas alfombras de Patricia Urquiola para cc-tapis. Una síntesis sin precedentes entre técnica antigua y gráficos contemporáneos. Patricia Urquiola nació en Oviedo en 1961. Actualmente trabaja y vive en Milán.
www.patriciaurquiola.com

Product Design

SHAPE

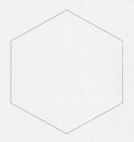 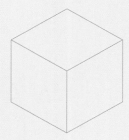 

COLORING

GRID

KAIWA

be.net/kaiwa

Iwaszczyszyn Kamil aka. K A I W A, is a graphic designer from Luxembourg.

Iwaszczyszyn Kamil aka. K A I W A, es un diseñador gráfico de Luxemburgo.

Hexagonetica Typeface (left page)

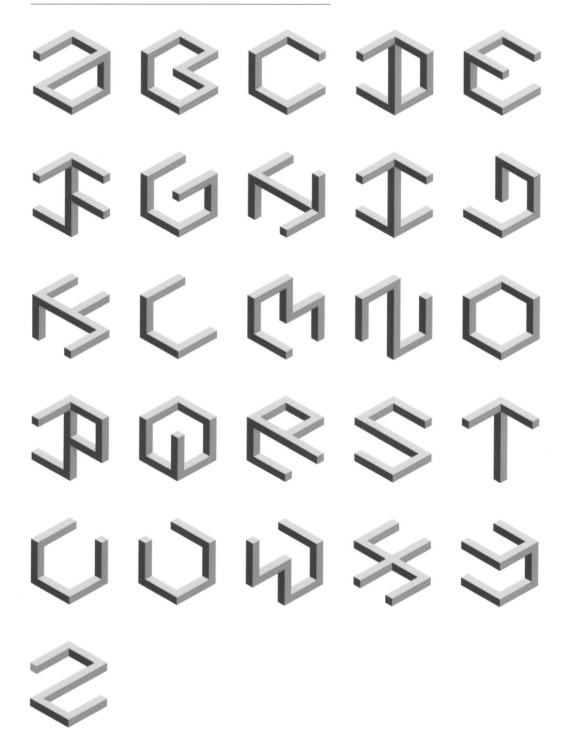

SHAPE

COLORS

GRID

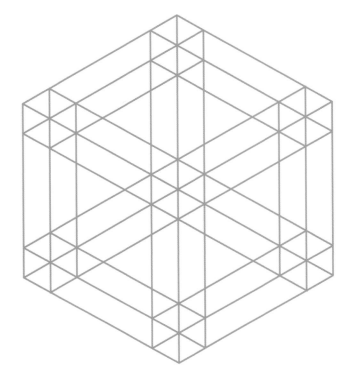

Project Name: Hexagonetica

The idea behind the creation of Hexagonetica was to draw an alphabet within a simple geometric form. Starting by making experiments with a square as basic-grid for the letters, concluding that there were not enough possibilities for what was intended.

Adding two corners and using the hexagon as grid for the letters, seamed as a good solution. This grid had to be respected and the shape of the letters had to derive from its possibilities.

The hexagon offered the best presupposition to turn the alphabet 3D by choosing complementary colors to simulate light and shadow. This exercise turned the alphabet into impossible objects, similar to those of M.C. Escher.

La idea detrás de la creación de Hexagonetica era dibujar un alfabeto dentro de una forma geométrica simple. Experimentando con un cuadrado como cuadrícula base para las letras, concluyendo que no había suficientes posibilidades para lo que se pretendía.

Añadí dos esquinas y utilicé el hexágono como cuadrícula para las letras, fue una buena solución. Esta cuadrícula tenía que ser respetada y la forma de las letras tenía que derivar de sus posibilidades.

El hexágono ofreció la mejor presuposición para convertir el alfabeto 3D mediante la elección de colores complementarios para simular la luz y la sombra. Este ejercicio convirtió el alfabeto en objetos imposibles, similares a los de M.C. Escher.

Typeface Design

TOTAL
RECALL

14.

DIRECTED BY
PAUL VERHOEVEN

RELEASE DATE
01.06.90
RUNNING TIME
113 MINUTES

BUDGET $60,000,000
BOX OFFICE $261,300,000

WWW.NICKBARCLAYDESIGNS.COM

Nicholas Barclay

www.nickbarclaydesigns.com

Nicholas Barclay is a designer in Sydney Australia.

He likes his work to be simple and informative and hold an idea. He likes to challenge himself to break something down to a simple form that looks like art work but also has a little information in it. Nicholas tries to keep his work fun and he likes people to have that "ah" moment when they understand what it is.

Nicholas Barclay es diseñador y vive en Sídney, Australia.

Le gusta que su trabajo sea sencillo, informativo y refleje una idea. Adora desafiarse a sí mismo para romper con todo y terminar en una forma simple con aspecto de obra de arte pero que además incluya algo de información. Nicholas intenta conservar la diversión de su trabajo y le encanta que la gente tenga ese momento "¡ah!" cuando descubren de qué se trata.

Total Recall (left page)

New York

01.

COUNTRY
UNITED STATES
POPULATION
8,405,837
COORDINATES
40°42'46"N
74°00'21"W

COLOURS
C0 M0 Y0 K8
C52 M0 Y80 K0
C0 M0 Y66 K0

WWW.NICKBARCLAYDESIGNS.COM

London

02.

WWW.NICKBARCLAYDESIGNS

COUNTRY
UNITED KINGDOM
POPULATION
8,416,535
COORDINATES
51°30'26"N
0°7'39"W

COLOURS
C0 M0 Y0 K8
C0 M0 Y6 K0
C15 M100 Y100 K0

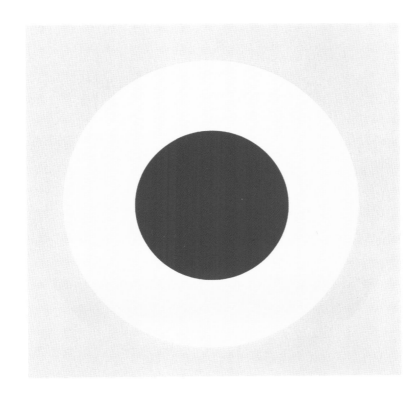

Rome
03.

San Francisco
04.

Berlin
07.

Madrid
08.

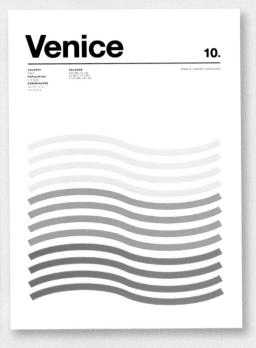

Cities, by Nicholas Barclay

Isolation 01.

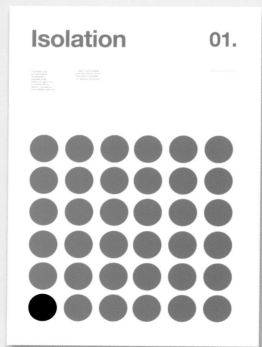

Withdrawal 02.

Hope 04.

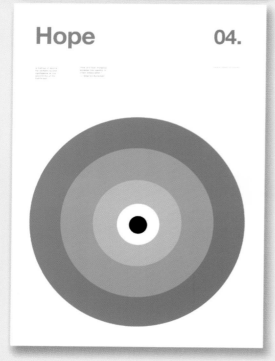

Clarity 05.

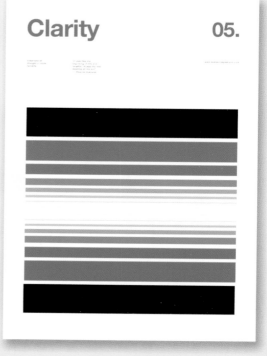

Confusion

06.

The state of
being bewildered
or unclear in
one's mind about
something.

"I don't know about other
people, but when I wake
up in the morning and
put my shoes on, I think,
Jesus Christ, now what?"
— Charles Bukowski

www.nickbarclaydesigns.com

Depression group, by Nicholas Barclay

Martini

Negroni

Daiquiri

Bellini

Margarita

Old-Fashio

Sazerac

1 SUGAR CUBE
2 1/2 OUNCES RYE WHISKY
3 DASHES PEYCHAUD'S BITTERS
1 DASH ANGOSTURA BITTERS
ABSINTHE
LEMON PEEL

Cosmopolitan

2 OUNCES VODKA
1 OUNCE COINTREAU
1 OUNCE CRANBERRY JUICE
1 OUNCE LIME JUICE

Manhattan

2 OUNCES RYE WHISKY
1 OUNCE ITALIAN VERMOUTH
2 DASHES ANGOSTURA BITTERS
TWIST OF ORANGE
MARASCHINO CHERRY

Bloody Mary

1 OUNCES VODKA
4 OUNCES TOMATO JUICE
1/2 TABLESPOON LEMON JUICE
1 SPLASH WORCESTERSHIRE SAUCE
3 TO 4 DASHES TABASCO
1 TEASPOON HORSERADISH
STALK OF CELERY

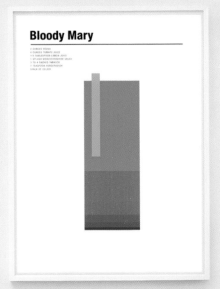

Emrys Architects

www.emrysarchitects.com

Photos by Alan Williams

Emrys Architects are an architectural practice based in Smithfield in London. Emrys are best known for creating value from underachieving existing buildings and sites, mainly working in the tight difficult spaces typical of Central London. Projects range from small quirky interventions to major new build developments for commercial, residential and educational clients.

Many of their projects are in listed buildings or conservation areas and Great James Street is a good example of fitting the new with the old. The 1720 Grade II listed terraced building with oak paneled board room leads through to a contemporary open-plan work space. Historical elements such as the silver vault have been incorporated into the new offices. Sustainability is a key consideration but can take many forms rather than just bolting on the latest technology – they place importance on recycling, re-use and longevity.

Recent projects include the conversion of an old tobacco pipe factory into residential flats and a 120,000 sq ft (11,150m2) mixed-used building in the heart of Soho,
central London – a contemporary building that had to sit within a sensitive conservation area.

Emrys Architects es un estudio de arquitectura ubicado en Smithfield, Londres. Emrys es conocido por revalorizar edificios y localizaciones existentes con potencial no explotado, trabajando principalmente en difíciles espacios ajustados comunes en el centro de Londres. Sus proyectos incluyen desde pequeñas intervenciones poco convencionales a nuevos desarrollos de construcción de gran envergadura para clientes comerciales, residenciales y educativos.

Muchos de sus proyectos se llevan a cabo en edificios protegidos o zonas de conservación, siendo Great James Street un buen ejemplo de adaptación entre lo nuevo y lo antiguo. En su edificio adosado protegido de Grado II de 1720, una sala panelada con tablas de madera de roble da paso a un contemporáneo espacio de trabajo de plano abierto. En las nuevas oficinas se han incorporado elementos históricos como la cúpula plateada. La sostenibilidad es un aspecto clave a tener en cuenta, pero puede conseguirse de muchas formas, no sólo recurriendo a las últimas tecnologías, también dando importancia al reciclaje, la reutilización y la larga duración.

Entre sus proyectos recientes encontramos la conversión de una antigua fábrica de pipas de fumar en apartamentos residenciales y un edificio de 11.150 m2 multiusos en el corazón del Soho, en el centro de Londres - un edificio contemporáneo que debía encajar en una sensible zona de conservación.

32 Great James Street by Emrys Architects

Project Name: 32 Great James Street

Client: GMS Estates

32 Great James Street comprises two five storey terraced townhouses built between 1720 and 1724 in Central London. The properties suffered bomb and fire damage during the Second World War and were patched-up shortly after with a series of rear extensions. Emrys Architects retained and enhanced the grandeur of the listed terrace and introduced an entirely new structure in the tight landlocked space to the rear to create a dramatic transition from old to the new. The structure is made up of a series of folded triangular plates that are self supporting when all panels are in place. These are retained by a continuous lightweight steel ring beam that ties all the panels together and prevents them from sliding away.

32 Great James Street está compuesto por dos casas adosadas con terraza de cinco plantas construidas entre 1720 y 1724 en el corazón de Londres. Las propiedades fueron objeto de bombardeos e incendios durante la Segunda Guerra Mundial y posteriormente fueron reformadas con una serie de extensiones en su parte posterior. Emrys Architects conservó y mejoró la grandeza de la terraza protegida e introdujo una estructura totalmente nueva en el ajustado espacio interior de la parte trasera para crear una transición drástica de lo antiguo a lo nuevo. La estructura está compuesta de una serie de placas triangulares plegadas que se soportan entre sí una vez colocados todos los paneles. Estos se fijan con una viga circular continua de acero ligero que une todos los paneles y evita que se deslicen.

Architectural project

Pedro Guerreiro

www.extrabold.studio

Pedro Guerreiro is founder and creative director of Extrabold, a small design studio in the beautiful city of Oporto, where he was born and raised as a designer.

He graduated in Comunication Design at Esad, and he soon discovered a passion for areas like Branding and Digital Media.

When he was studying graphic design, he tried to work with different media, and explored the skills of each one, from the digital to the silkscreen printing. Pedro had the chance to experiment and test freely, which lead him to take a very broad approach in design.

After he start working as a designer, he realized that the way brands communicate defines their value, so design is an essential tool for positioning and establishing a brand identity and improve both image and concept level, therefore, creativity is the solution for better strategic thinking and problem solving.

Pedro Guerreiro es el fundador y director creativo de Extrabold, un pequeño estudio de diseño situado en la preciosa ciudad de Oporto, lugar en el que nació y creció como diseñador.

Pedro se graduó en Diseño de Comunicación en la ESAD y pronto descubrió su pasión por campos como el branding y los medios digitales.

Mientras estudiaba diseño gráfico, intentó trabajar con diferentes medios, desde medios digitales a serigrafía, explorando las capacidades de cada uno de ellos. Tuvo la oportunidad de experimentar y realizar pruebas de manera libre, lo que le permitió adquirir una perspectiva muy amplia del diseño.

Tras comenzar a trabajar como diseñador se dio cuenta de que el modo en que las marcas se comunican define su valor, por lo que el diseño es una herramienta esencial para lograr y establecer una identidad de marca, además de para mejorar tanto su imagen como el nivel conceptual, de ahí que la creatividad sea la solución para implementar un pensamiento estratégico y resolver problemas.

Beijing design week Poster (left page)

Beijing design week Poster by Pedro Guerreiro

Melissa Zambrana

www.mz-graphisme.com

Melissa Zambrana is a French Graphic Designer, co-founder of the Agency La Cocotte. She has been working in Print and Web Design, from France to Sydney, with only one thing in her mind: making each project, little or big, a unique creation born from a strong concept.

What defines her work is simplicity, minimalism and detail.

Melissa Zambrana es una diseñadora gráfica francesa, cofundadora de la agencia La Cocotte. Melissa ha trabajado en los campos del diseño web e impreso, desde Francia hasta Sídney, con sólo un objetivo en la cabeza: hacer de cada proyecto, pequeño o grande, una creación única surgida de un concepto sólido.

Su trabajo está definido por la simplicidad, el minimalismo y el detalle.

Choreographic design (left page)

Agapé
DANCE STUDIO

Project Name: Choreographic design

Client: Agapé

As a dancer, I am interested in the relation between choreography and graphic design.
Geometric shapes, lines, spaces and directions are the essential components of a good creation. I decided to recreate the notion of rythm and repetition wich are inherent to the idea of movement by decomposing the image. Jerky movement, repeated movement, continuous movement.
My aim is to represent the movement in a space-time dimension, through a frozen photography.

Como bailarina, estoy interesada en la relación entre la coreografía y el diseño gráfico.
Las formas geométricas, las líneas, los espacios y las direcciones son los componentes esenciales de una buena creación. He decidido recrear la noción de ritmo y repetición, inherentes a la idea de movimiento, descomponiendo la imagen. Movimiento errático, movimiento repetido, movimiento continuado.
Mi objetivo es representar el movimiento en una dimensión espacio-tiempo, a través de una fotografía congelada.

Poster Series

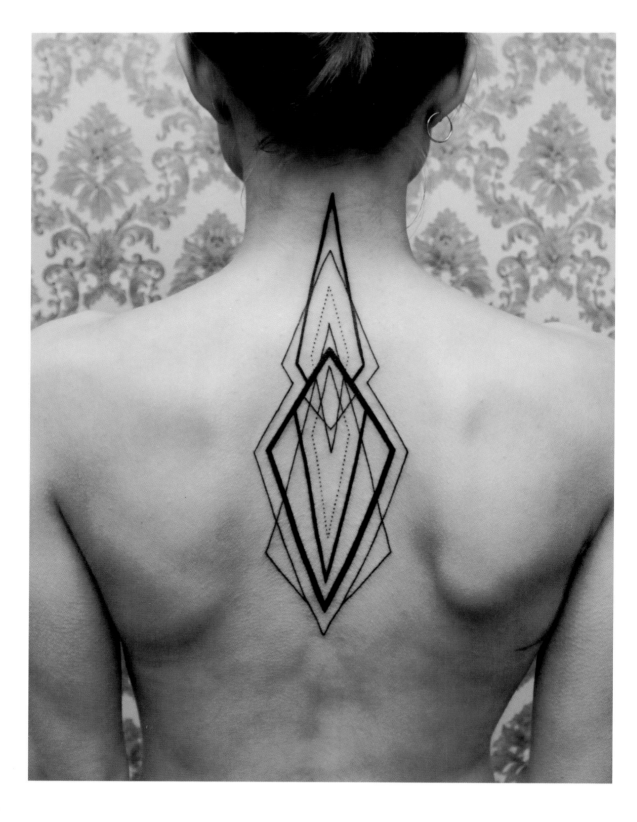

Chaim Machlev

www.dotstolines.com

Chaim Machlev started tattooing 4 years ago, in spring 2012. His first tattoo was on a friend that was kind enough to let him practice on her doing a little sea star that looked actually pretty good. Chaim said that his second tattoo was horrible actually. "It is funny to talk about the first approach to tattooing because when it comes to reality and you hold your tattoo machine for the first time in your hand and aim it towards someone you don't really know where to gain the confident to actually do it so you really find yourself trusting just instincts." And those instincts become habits during the time and the experience. He was born and raised in Tel Aviv, Israel, he moved to Berlin to learn how to tattoo.

Chaim Machlev comenzó a tatuar hace 4 años, durante la primavera de 2012. Su primer tatuaje se lo realizó a una amiga lo suficientemente amable para dejarle practicar con ella haciendo una pequeña estrella de mar que quedó bastante bien. Chaim afirma que su segundo tatuaje en realidad fue horrible. "Es divertido hablar del primer acercamiento a los tatuajes porque cuando se convierte en realidad y coges la máquina de tatuar y la diriges hacia alguien por primera vez no sabes muy bien cómo confiar en hacerlo de verdad así que simplemente confías en instintos." Y esos instintos se convierten en hábitos con tiempo y experiencia. Nació y creció en Tel Aviv, Israel, y se trasladó a Berlín para aprender a tatuar.

Untitled (left page)

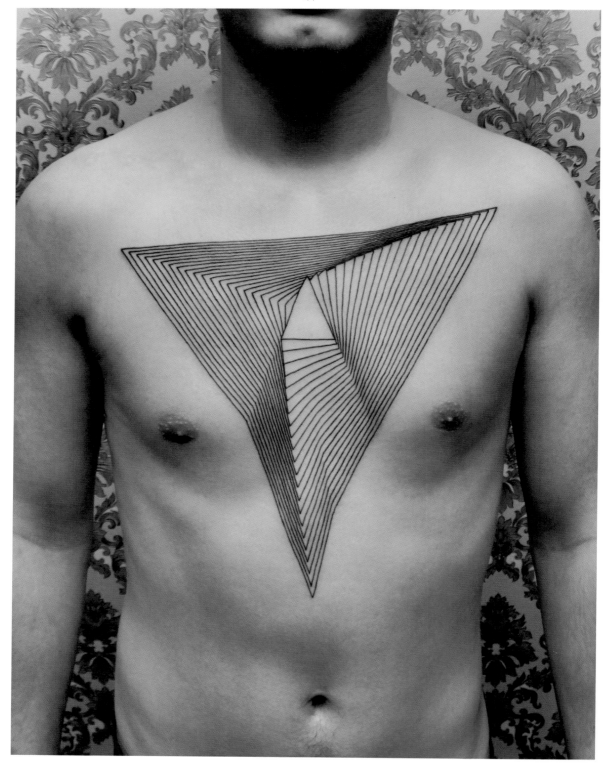

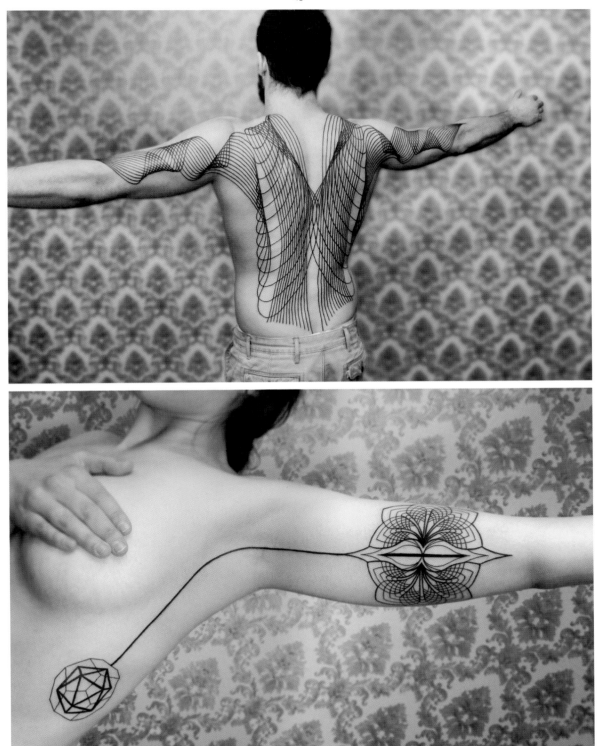

Tattos by Chaim Machlev

Tattos by Chaim Machlev

Tattos by Chaim Machlev

Axel Peemoeller

www.axelpeemoeller.com

Axel Peemoeller works and lives in New York City, his work is driven by design and ideas. His work over the last 2 decades has been internationally recognised and awarded. Axel Peemöller is his own studio a design consultancy based in New York, expertise in branding/identity/strategy as well as brand and product development, environmental design, signage, event-exhibition design, photo and videography direction, editorial design, web an app design and packaging.

Axel Peemoeller trabaja y vive en Nueva York, y su trabajo está dirigido por el diseño y las ideas. Su obra de las dos últimas décadas ha recibido reconocimiento y premios a nivel internacional. Axel Peemöller es su estudio, una consultoría de diseño situada en Nueva York, especializada en branding/ identidad/estrategia y desarrollo de marcas y productos, diseño mediomabiental, diseño de carteles, diseño para exposiciones-eventos, dirección fotográfica y videográfica, diseño editorial, diseño web y de aplicaciones y diseño de envoltorios.

Apex Longboards (left page)

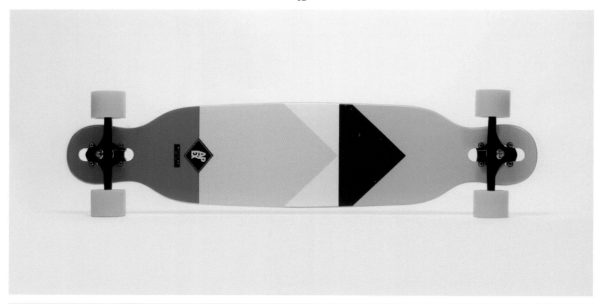

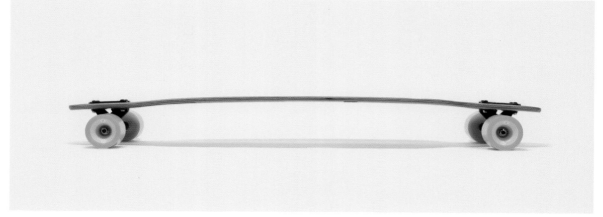

Project Name: Apex Longboards

Client: Apex

For the identity and design of the APEX
longboards I drew inspiration of bauhaus shapes
and nautical flags.

*Para la identidad y el diseño de los longboards de
APEX me inspiré en los dibujos del bauhaus y de
las banderas náuticas.*

Skateboard design

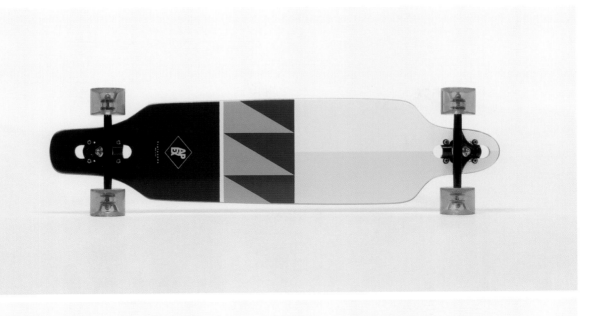

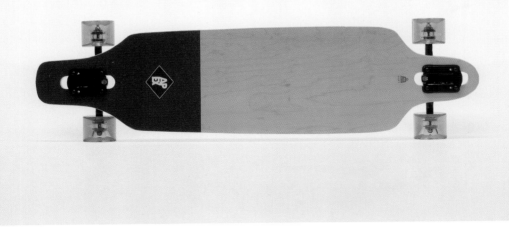

Apex Longboards by Axel Peemoeller

it is
what
it is

N°1

**Linus Lohoff
Art Direction &
Photography**

Linus Lohoff is a multi-disciplined
Art Director & Photographer from
Germany with brazilian roots who
lives in Barcelona, Spain. He has over
six years of professional experience
in visual communication like editorial
design, photography, typography,

storytelling, infographics, branding
and corporate identity – print and
digital. His passion is photography
which luckily brought him to work
with magazines and galleries. He is
available for any assignments. Feel
free to contact him:

+34 603 758 448
info@linuslohoff.com
c/Montsiò 17-2
08002 Barcelona, Spain

www.linuslohoff.com

Linus Lohoff

www.linuslohoff.com

Linus Lohoff is a multi-disciplined Art Director &
Photographer from Germany with brazilian roots who
recently settled down in Spain. Currently he is working
with national and international clients across an open
range of fields while working for Vasava, a design agency
based in Barcelona.

*Linus Lohoff es un director artístico y fotógrafo
multidisciplinar alemán con raíces brasileñas que
recientemente se ha asentado en España. En la actualidad
trabaja para clientes tanto nacionales como internacionales
en una amplia selección de campos a la vez que lo hace para
Vasava, una agencia de diseño con sede en Barcelona.*

It is what it is (left page)

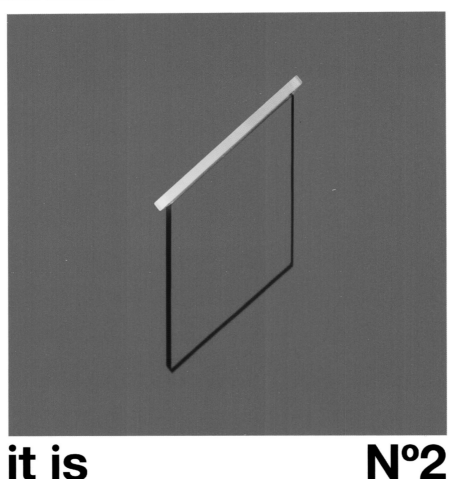

it is
what
it is

Nº2

Linus Lohoff
Art Direction &
Photography

Linus Lohoff is a multi-disciplined Art Director & Photographer from Germany with brazilian roots who lives in Barcelona, Spain. He has over six years of professional experience in visual communication like editorial design, photography, typography, storytelling, infographics, branding and corporate identity – print and digital. His passion is photography which luckily brought him to work with magazines and galleries. He is available for any assignments. Feel free to contact him:

+34 603 758 448
info@linuslohoff.com
c/Montsió 17-2
08002 Barcelona, Spain

www.linuslohoff.com

it is
what
it is

Nº3

**Linus Lohoff
Art Direction &
Photography**

Linus Lohoff is a multi-disciplined Art Director & Photographer from Germany with brazilian roots who lives in Barcelona, Spain. He has over six years of professional experience in visual communication like editorial design, photography, typography,

storytelling, infographics, branding and corporate identity – print and digital. His passion is photography which luckily brought him to work with magazines and galleries. He is available for any assignments. Feel free to contact him:

+34 603 758 448
info@linuslohoff.com
c/Montsiò 17-2
08002 Barcelona, Spain

www.linuslohoff.com

It is what it is by Linus Lohoff

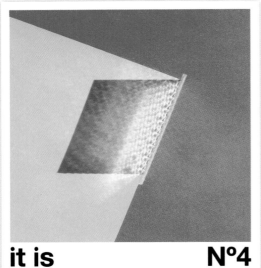

it is what it is

Nº4

**Linus Lohoff
Art Direction &
Photography**

Linus Lohoff is a multi-disciplined Art Director & Photographer from Germany with brazilian roots who lives in Barcelona, Spain. He has over six years of professional experience in visual communication like editorial design, photography, typography,

storytelling, infographics, branding and corporate identity – print and digital. His passion is photography which luckily brought him to work with magazines and galleries. He is available for any assignments. Feel free to contact him:

+34 003 758 448
info@linuslohoff.com
c/Montlló 17-2
08002 Barcelona, Spain

www.linuslohoff.com

it is what it is

Nº5

**Linus Lohoff
Art Direction &
Photography**

Linus Lohoff is a multi-disciplined Art Director & Photographer from Germany with brazilian roots who lives in Barcelona, Spain. He has over six years of professional experience in visual communication like editorial design, photography, typography,

storytelling, infographics, branding and corporate identity – print and digital. His passion is photography which luckily brought him to work with magazines and galleries. He is available for any assignments. Feel free to contact him:

+34 003 758 448
info@linuslohoff.com
c/Montlló 17-2
08002 Barcelona, Spain

www.linuslohoff.com

it is what it is

Nº6

**Linus Lohoff
Art Direction &
Photography**

Linus Lohoff is a multi-disciplined Art Director & Photographer from Germany with brazilian roots who lives in Barcelona, Spain. He has over six years of professional experience in visual communication like editorial design, photography, typography,

storytelling, infographics, branding and corporate identity – print and digital. His passion is photography which luckily brought him to work with magazines and galleries. He is available for any assignments. Feel free to contact him:

+34 003 758 448
info@linuslohoff.com
c/Montlló 17-2
08002 Barcelona, Spain

www.linuslohoff.com

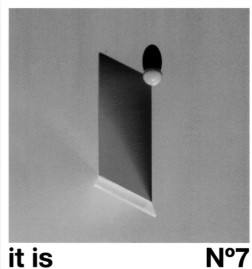

it is what it is

Nº7

**Linus Lohoff
Art Direction &
Photography**

Linus Lohoff is a multi-disciplined Art Director & Photographer from Germany with brazilian roots who lives in Barcelona, Spain. He has over six years of professional experience in visual communication like editorial design, photography, typography,

storytelling, infographics, branding and corporate identity – print and digital. His passion is photography which luckily brought him to work with magazines and galleries. He is available for any assignments. Feel free to contact him:

+34 503 758 448
info@linuslohoff.com
c/Montlló 17-2
08002 Barcelona, Spain

www.linuslohoff.com

it is what it is · Nº8

Linus Lohoff
Art Direction &
Photography

it is what it is · Nº9

Linus Lohoff
Art Direction &
Photography

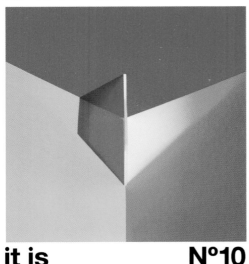

it is what it is · Nº10

Linus Lohoff
Art Direction &
Photography

Project Name: It is what it is

Client: Self publication

This series of images depicting abstract photoillustrations with the formal means of form, color, material and light represents my profession of art direction and photography. »It is what it is« removes all contextual meaning, trying to stand on their own and allowing the spectator to place their own thoughts onto it, if they so wished. These pictures are combined in a constantly enriched poster series as self publication and promotion of »Linus Lohoff – Art Direction & Photography«.

Esta serie de imágenes que muestran fotoilustraciones abstractas por medio de formas, colores, materiales y luces representa mi profesión en el ámbito de la dirección artística y la fotografía. La serie »It is what it is« (Es lo que es) elimina cualquier significado contextual, intentando sustentarse por sí misma y permitiendo al espectador tener sus propios pensamientos, si así lo desea. Estas imágenes se combinan en una serie de pósteres con adiciones continuadas en forma de autopublicación y promoción de »Linus Lohoff – Art Direction & Photography«.

Poster Series

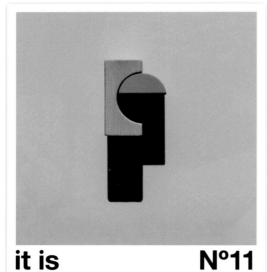

it is
what
it is

N°11

**Linus Lohoff
Art Direction &
Photography**

Linus Lohoff is a multi-disciplined Art Director & Photographer from Germany with brazilian roots who lives in Barcelona, Spain. He has over six years of professional experience in visual communication like editorial design, photography, typography,

storytelling, infographics, branding and corporate identity – print and digital. His passion is photography which luckily brought him to work with magazines and galleries. He is available for any assignments. Feel free to contact him:

+34 603 758 448
info@linuslohoff.com
c/Montsió 17-2
08002 Barcelona, Spain

www.linuslohoff.com

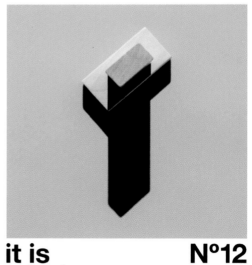

it is
what
it is

N°12

**Linus Lohoff
Art Direction &
Photography**

Linus Lohoff is a multi-disciplined Art Director & Photographer from Germany with brazilian roots who lives in Barcelona, Spain. He has over six years of professional experience in visual communication like editorial design, photography, typography,

storytelling, infographics, branding and corporate identity – print and digital. His passion is photography which luckily brought him to work with magazines and galleries. He is available for any assignments. Feel free to contact him:

+34 603 758 448
info@linuslohoff.com
c/Montsió 17-2
08002 Barcelona, Spain

www.linuslohoff.com

it is
what
it is

N°13

**Linus Lohoff
Art Direction &
Photography**

Linus Lohoff is a multi-disciplined Art Director & Photographer from Germany with brazilian roots who lives in Barcelona, Spain. He has over six years of professional experience in visual communication like editorial design, photography, typography,

storytelling, infographics, branding and corporate identity – print and digital. His passion is photography which luckily brought him to work with magazines and galleries. He is available for any assignments. Feel free to contact him:

+34 603 758 448
info@linuslohoff.com
c/Montsió 17-2
08002 Barcelona, Spain

www.linuslohoff.com

it is
what
it is

N°14

**Linus Lohoff
Art Direction &
Photography**

Linus Lohoff is a multi-disciplined Art Director & Photographer from Germany with brazilian roots who lives in Barcelona, Spain. He has over six years of professional experience in visual communication like editorial design, photography, typography,

storytelling, infographics, branding and corporate identity – print and digital. His passion is photography which luckily brought him to work with magazines and galleries. He is available for any assignments. Feel free to contact him:

+34 603 758 448
info@linuslohoff.com
c/Montsió 17-2
08002 Barcelona, Spain

www.linuslohoff.com

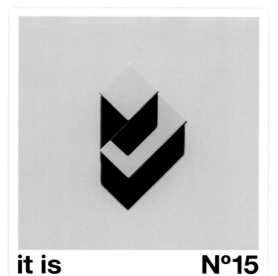

it is
what
it is

N°15

**Linus Lohoff
Art Direction &
Photography**

Linus Lohoff is a multi-disciplined Art Director & Photographer from Germany with brazilian roots who lives in Barcelona, Spain. He has over six years of professional experience in visual communication like editorial design, photography, typography,

storytelling, infographics, branding and corporate identity – print and digital. His passion is photography which luckily brought him to work with magazines and galleries. He is available for any assignments. Feel free to contact him:

+34 603 756 448
info@linuslohoff.com
c/Montaló 17-2
08002 Barcelona, Spain

www.linuslohoff.com

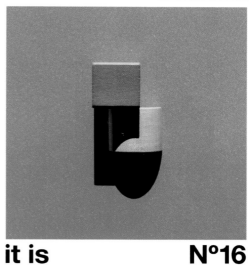

it is
what
it is

N°16

**Linus Lohoff
Art Direction &
Photography**

Linus Lohoff is a multi-disciplined Art Director & Photographer from Germany with brazilian roots who lives in Barcelona, Spain. He has over six years of professional experience in visual communication like editorial design, photography, typography,

storytelling, infographics, branding and corporate identity – print and digital. His passion is photography which luckily brought him to work with magazines and galleries. He is available for any assignments. Feel free to contact him:

+34 603 756 448
info@linuslohoff.com
c/Montaló 17-2
08002 Barcelona, Spain

www.linuslohoff.com

it is
what
it is

N°17

**Linus Lohoff
Art Direction &
Photography**

Linus Lohoff is a multi-disciplined Art Director & Photographer from Germany with brazilian roots who lives in Barcelona, Spain. He has over six years of professional experience in visual communication like editorial design, photography, typography,

storytelling, infographics, branding and corporate identity – print and digital. His passion is photography which luckily brought him to work with magazines and galleries. He is available for any assignments. Feel free to contact him:

+34 603 756 448
info@linuslohoff.com
c/Montaló 17-2
08002 Barcelona, Spain

www.linuslohoff.com

it is
what
it is

N°18

**Linus Lohoff
Art Direction &
Photography**

Linus Lohoff is a multi-disciplined Art Director & Photographer from Germany with brazilian roots who lives in Barcelona, Spain. He has over six years of professional experience in visual communication like editorial design, photography, typography,

storytelling, infographics, branding and corporate identity – print and digital. His passion is photography which luckily brought him to work with magazines and galleries. He is available for any assignments. Feel free to contact him:

+34 603 756 448
info@linuslohoff.com
c/Montaló 17-2
08002 Barcelona, Spain

www.linuslohoff.com

It is what it is by Linus Lohoff

it is
what
it is

Nº19

Linus Lohoff
Art Direction &
Photography

Linus Lohoff is a multi-disciplined Art Director & Photographer from Germany with brazilian roots who lives in Barcelona, Spain. He has over six years of professional experience in visual communication like editorial design, photography, typography, storytelling, infographics, branding and corporate identity – print and digital. His passion is photography which luckily brought him to work with magazines and galleries. He is available for any assignments. Feel free to contact him:

+34 603 758 448
info@linuslohoff.com
c/Montsió 17-2
08002 Barcelona, Spain

www.linuslohoff.com

it is
what
it is

Nº20

Linus Lohoff
Art Direction &
Photography

Linus Lohoff is a multi-disciplined
Art Director & Photographer from
Germany with brazilian roots who
lives in Barcelona, Spain. He has over
six years of professional experience
in visual communication like editorial
design, photography, typography,

storytelling, infographics, branding
and corporate identity – print and
digital. His passion is photography
which luckily brought him to work
with magazines and galleries. He is
available for any assignments. Feel
free to contact him:

+34 603 758 448
info@linuslohoff.com
c/Montsió 17-2
08002 Barcelona, Spain

www.linuslohoff.com

It is what it is by Linus Lohoff

Kerby Rosanes

www.kerbyrosanes.com
instagram: kerbyrosanes

Kerby Rosanes is an illustrator based in the Philippines working mainly with multi liners to magically illustrate his intricate "doodle" world. At 25, Kerby has worked with various global brands and has already published five books including the New York Times best-seller, Animorphia. When not at his drawing desk, he travels the world to find new ideas and inspirations.

Kerby Rosanes es un ilustrador residente en Filipinas que trabaja principalmente con estilógrafos para ilustrar de manera mágica su complejo mundo de "garabatos". Con sólo 25 años, Kerby ha trabajado ya para varias marcas internacionales y ha publicado cinco libros, entre ellos Animorphia, clasificado como best-seller por The New York Times. Cuando no está en su mesa dibujando, viaja por todo el mundo en busca de nuevas ideas e inspiraciones.

Deer (left page)

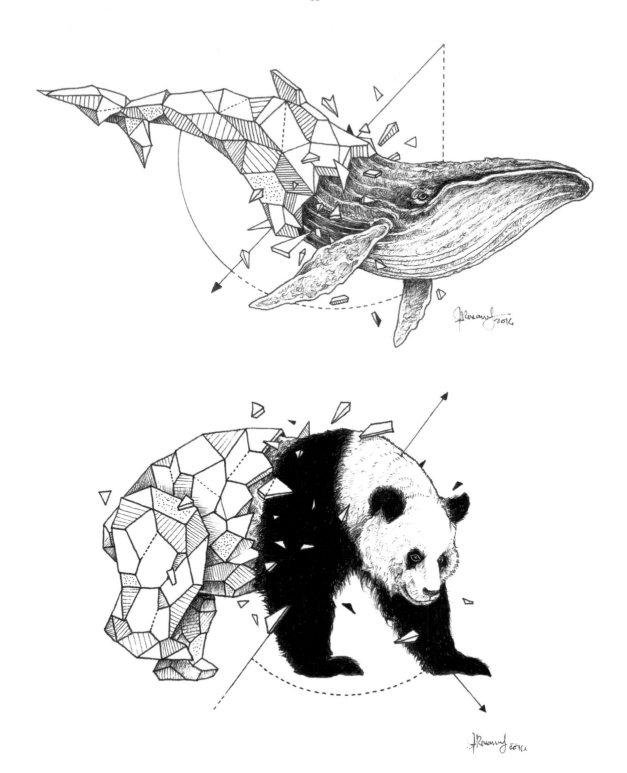

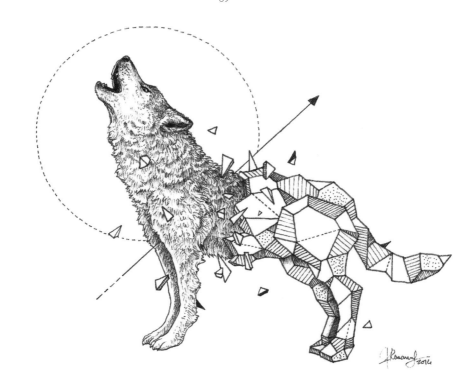

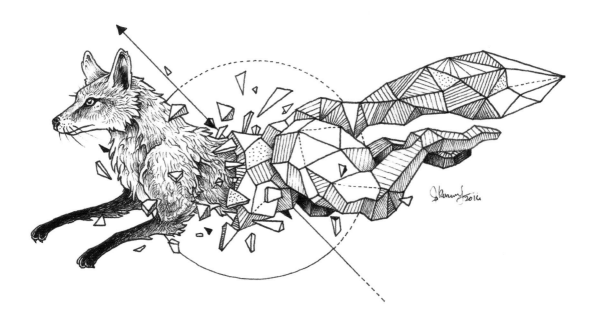

Geometric Beasts by Kerby Rosanes

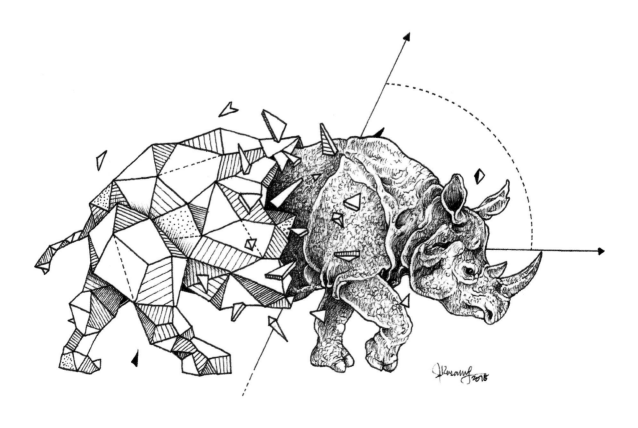

Project Name: Geometric Beasts

The "Geometric Beasts" collection is a series of ink drawings by Kerby Rosanes depicting his own interpretation of one's struggle on breaking away from societal norms and just be who we truly are as unique individuals. Represented by animals escaping out of their geometric forms, the series encourages us to unleash the "beast" within us - risk taker, wild, free and adventurous.

La colección "Geometric Beasts" (Bestias geométricas) es una de las series de dibujos a tinta de Kerby Rosanes, una interpretación propia de cómo salirse de las normas de la sociedad y ser quien realmente somos como individuos únicos. Representada mediante animales que escapan de sus formas geométricas, esta serie nos anima a sacar la "bestia" que llevamos dentro, salvaje, libre, aventurera y a la que le gusta correr riesgos.

Drawings

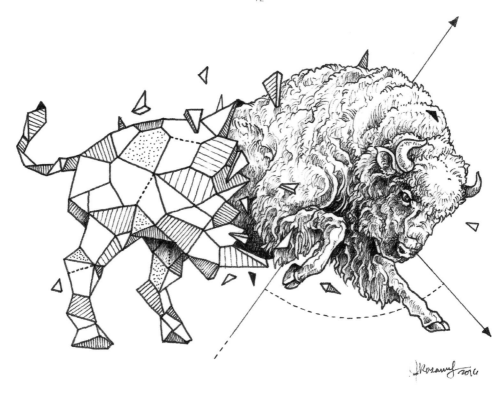

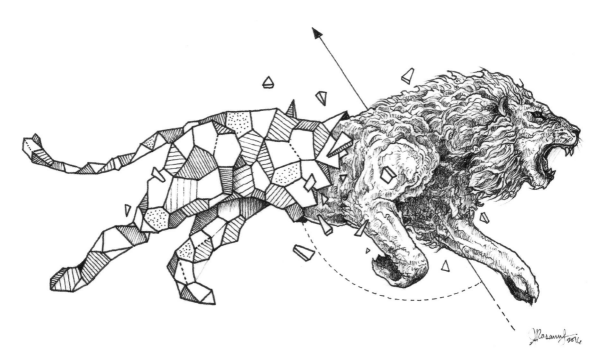

Geometric Beasts by Kerby Rosanes

Ray Oranges

www.ray-oranges.com
instagram: ray_oranges

Ray Oranges is an illustrator based in Florence.

There is something special about Ray's artwork: he has the ability tell a whole story with just a few well chosen details. The absence of cluttering matter, enhanced by the mastery use of long shadows and bursts of light creates an emotional response in the viewer.

Ray's message is always strong and to the point, although never aggressive. Ray's artwork doesn't aim at shouting louder than its surroundings – it doesn't have to. The skilful use of full and empty spaces within the composition, with a predominance of the latter, is open territory for the viewer to fill the space with feelings and experiences; Ray aims at creating a meaningful dialogue with the viewer rather than establishing a relationship of command.

Ray Oranges es un ilustrador residente en Florencia.

Su obra tiene algo de especial: Ray tiene la capacidad de contar una historia completa con sólo unos cuantos detalles bien elegidos. La ausencia de materia de sobrecarga, mejorada mediante el uso magistral de largas sombras y ráfagas de luz crea una respuesta emocional en el espectador.

El mensaje de Ray siempre es firme y directo, aunque nunca agresivo. La obra de Ray no pretende gritar más alto que lo que la rodea, no debe hacerlo. Su habilidoso uso de los espacios llenos y vacíos dentro de la composición, con predominio de estos últimos, ofrece al espectador un territorio que puede rellenarse libremente de sensaciones y experiencias. Más que establecer una relación de mando, Ray busca crear un diálogo significativo con el espectador.

Abstract architecture (left page)

Abstract architecture by Ray Oranges

Life-Home-Love-Time by Ray Oranges and Federico Landini

Project Name: Life-Home-Love-Time

This project is a collaboration between Federico Landini and Ray Oranges.

Este proyecto es una colaboración entre Federico Landini y Ray Oranges.

Type design

Emotional Layers by Ray Oranges

Interharmony by Ray Oranges

Quantum by Ray Oranges

Norme & Tributi Mese by Ray Oranges

Abstract architecture by Ray Oranges

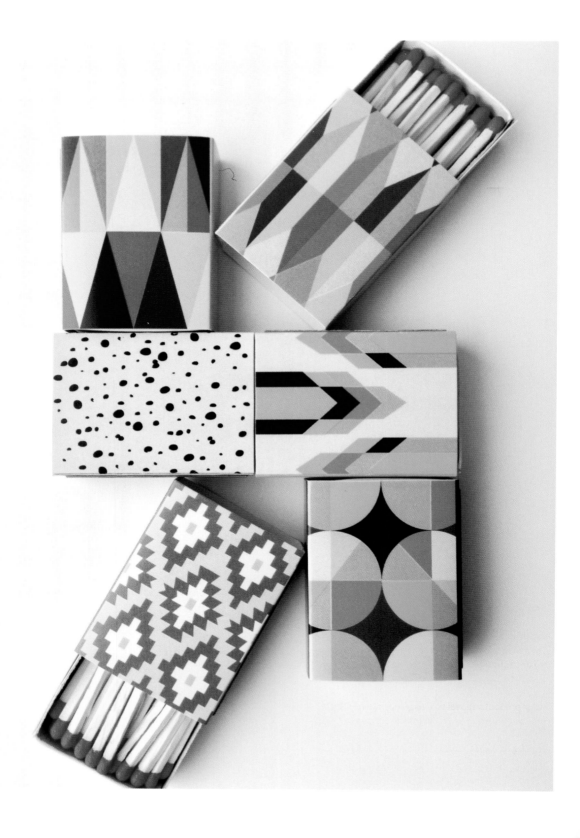

BelloPop

www.bellopop.com
www.etsy.com/ca/shop/BelloPop

BelloPop is a company dedicated to designing and bringing to life products that can make great gifts, unique home decorations and can just generally brighten someone's day. "We create everyday items that look stylish and fun".

Andreina Bello is the Creative Director behind BelloPop and her designs are generally a playful combination between geometric shapes and unexpected colour combinations. It's a well known fact that colour can have a big impact on people's moods and feelings and we aim to evoke the playfulness side of it.

"Our products appeal to design enthusiasts and consumers with an appreciation for charming paper goods".

BelloPop es una compañía dedicada al diseño y animación de productos que pueden convertirse en un excelente regalo, elementos de decoración del hogar únicos y que, en general, pueden iluminar el día de cualquier persona. "Creamos objetos cotidianos con un aspecto elegante y divertido."

Andreina Bello es la directora creativa de BelloPop y sus diseños son en general una alegre mezcla de formas geométricas y combinaciones de color inesperadas. Es de sobra sabido que el color puede influir enormemente en nuestro ánimo y sensaciones, por lo que intentamos evocar su lado más gracioso.

"Nuestros productos atraen a los entusiastas del diseño y a consumidores que saben apreciar los artículos cautivadores."

Matchbox (left page)

Matchbox, by BelloPop

Rebecca Finell

www.finell.co

Rebecca Finell previously founded Boon Inc., serving as the president, principal designer and chief brand strategist for the leading global innovator in the baby product industry. In January 2013, she launched Finell, a designer and manufacturer of neo luxe housewares and handbags. Finell is known to create new utilities and exciting products that redefine modern design. Rebecca Finell has received international design recognition, the attention of top luxury stores, museums, and ongoing features in high-profile press and Hollywood movies.

Rebecca Finell fundó en primer lugar Boon Inc., en la que desempeñaba funciones de presidenta, diseñadora principal y encargada de la estrategia de marca para esta innovadora empresa líder a nivel mundial del sector de los productos para bebés. En enero de 2013, lanzó Finell, compañía dedicada al diseño y fabricación de artículos para el hogar y bolsos de neolujo. Finell es conocida por crear nuevas utilidades y emocionantes productos que redefinen el diseño moderno. Los diseños de Rebecca Finell han recibido reconocimiento internacional, la atención de establecimientos de lujo de primer nivel y museos y apariciones en películas de Hollywood o artículos de prensa de perfil elevado.

Finell's handbag (left page)

Project Name: Finell's handbag

Finell's patented handbag designs are inspired by origami which create unique architectural forms that are also very functional. They are made from fine US leather and lined with microfiber interiors.

Los diseños de bolsos patentados de Finell están inspirados en el origami, creando formas arquitectónicas únicas a la vez que funcionales. Están fabricados en refinada piel de EE.UU. y cuentan con interiores de microfibra.

Handbag designs

Isabella Conticello

www.behance.net/IsabellaConticello

Isabella Conticello is graphic designer and illustrator. Her style is clear, simple and colorful, dominated by graphic minimalism and research geometric composition. She currently works as a freelance graphic designer and illustrator in Milan.

Isabella Conticello es diseñadora gráfica e ilustradora. Su estilo es claro, sencillo y colorido, está dominado por el minimalismo gráfico y busca composiciones geométricas. Actualmente trabaja como diseñadora gráfica e ilustradora independiente en Milán.

• **A GEO A DAY** • (left page)

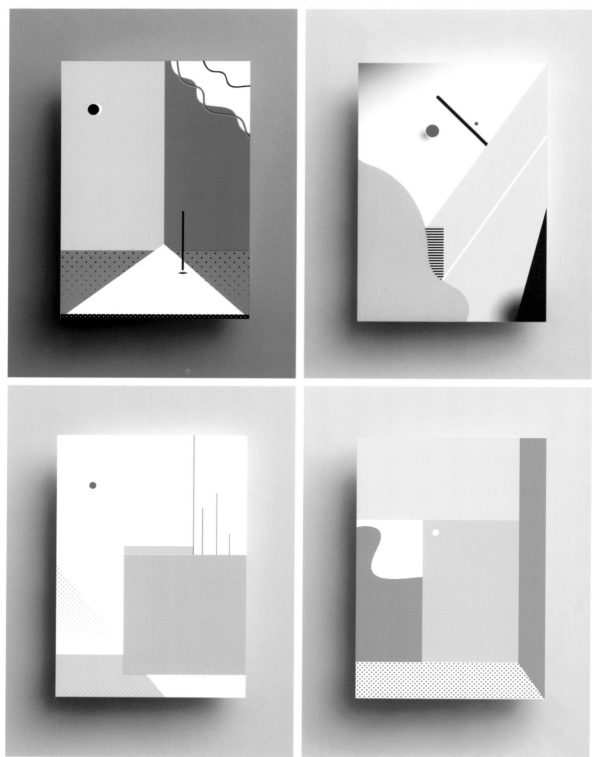

• **A GEO A DAY** ▪, by Isabella Conticello

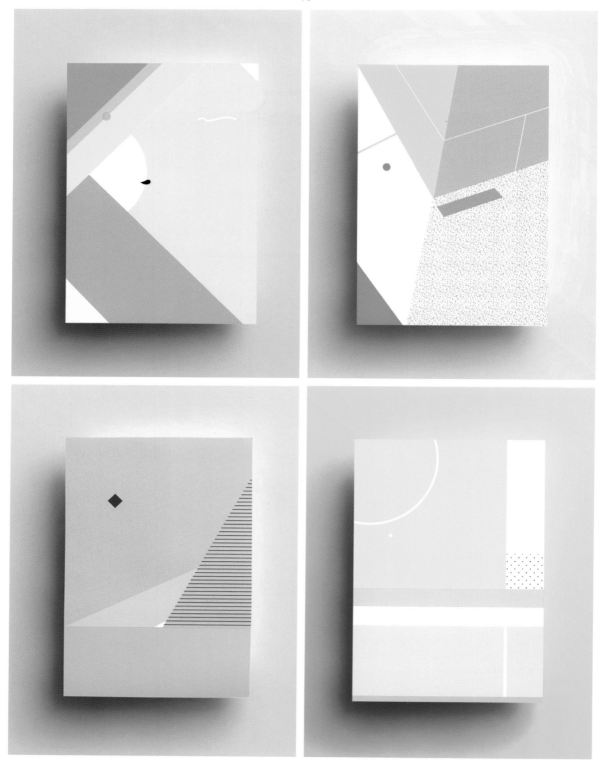

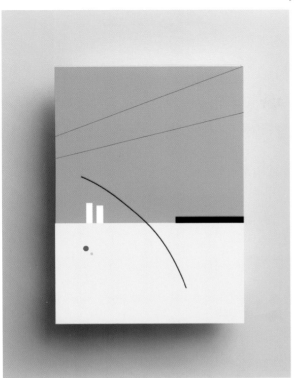

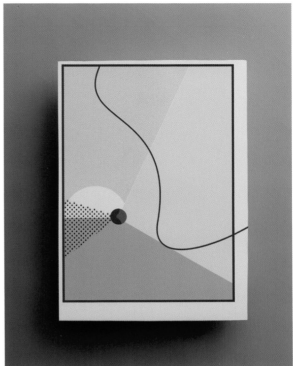

Project Name: • A GEO A DAY ▪

Client: Personal project

A geometry a day is a personal diary. "Is the visual story of what happens to me every day, the story of everything that happens in my unique and unforgettable day. The project was born in the Valentine's Day 2015, and continues every day since then. My style and my projects and works are simple, and inspired by humanity and the nature and the city around us … everything is transformed into graphic …"

"A geometry a day" (Un día, una forma geométrica) es un diario personal. "Se trata de la historia visual de lo que ocurre en mi día a día, la historia de todo lo que sucede en mis únicos e inolvidables días. El proyecto nació el Día de San Valentín de 2015 y continúa cada día desde entonces. Mi estilo, mis proyectos y mis trabajos son sencillos y están inspirados en la humanidad, la naturaleza, la ciudad que nos rodea… Todo se transforma en un gráfico…"

Illustration

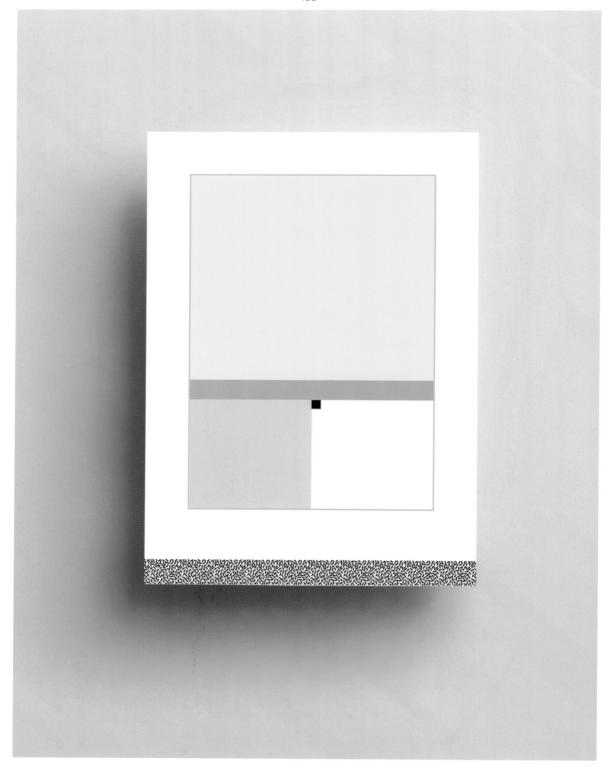

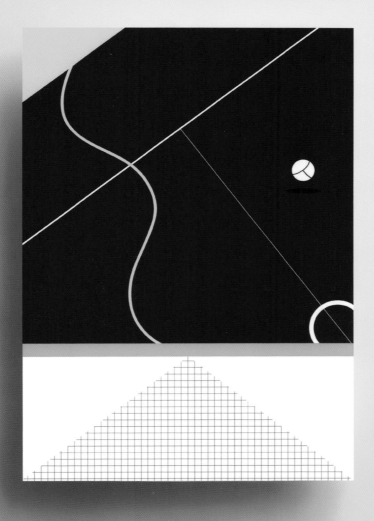

• **A GEO A DAY** ▪, by Isabella Conticello

One Darnley Road

www.onedarnleyroad.com

One Darnley Road are a multidisciplinary creative agency based in Hackney, East London. Founded in 2007 by a collective of experienced creatives and digital experts with a shared love of intelligent ideas and meticulous craft, they build compelling brand stories – beautifully told, both on and offline.

One Darnley Road es una agencia creativa multidisciplinar con sede en Hackney, en la zona este de Londres. Fundada en 2007 por un grupo de creativos experimentados y expertos en medios digitales amantes de las ideas inteligentes y el trabajo meticuloso, desarrollan atractivas historias de marca, contadas de manera hermosa, tanto dentro como fuera de la red.

Soap packaging (left page)

Project Name: London Fields Soap Company

Client: London Fields Soap Company

Launching as an artisan brand, London Fields Soap Company required an identity that complimented their range of organic, beautiful products. Their ambition is to "bring back the bar", with soaps that are good for the skin and the environment, all made locally by hand in Hackney, East London.

Presentada como una marca artesanal, London Fields Soap Company requería una identidad que complementara su gama de productos orgánicos bonitos. Su ambición es "volver a la pastilla", con jabones respetuosos con la piel y el medio ambiente, fabricados a mano a nivel local en Hackney, en la zona este de Londres.

Branding and Packaging Design

BUSK

Singer Songwriter Festival
13–14.06.2014
Bolzano
Bozen

Design: Thomas Kronbichler, Max Edelberg

Città di Bolzano
Stadt Bozen

Assessorato alla Convivenza e alle Politiche Sociali
Deutsches Amt für aktives Zusammenleben

13+14.06.2014 Bolzano Bozen

franz
magazine
.com

Studio Mut

www.studiomut.com

Studio Mut is a graphic design studio founded by Thomas Kronbichler and Martin Kerschbaumer, based in Bolzano, Italy. The studio specialises in identity, print, editorial and web design for clients spanning art, culture and commerce. They seek for simple and powerful solutions, bold aesthetics and surprising outputs across all platforms. Their work has been described as both playful and serious, and they strive to keep the balance.

It's Nice That writes that their work is «abstracted to just the right level and in a colour palette dialled up to 11», and AIGA Magazine calls them «Italy's Friendliest Graphic Design Studio».

Studio Mut es un estudio de diseño gráfico fundado por Thomas Kronbichler y Martin Kerschbaumer situado en Bolzano, Italia. El estudio está especializado en diseño de identidades, impresiones, editorial y web para clientes dedicados al arte, la cultura y el comercio. Su objetivo es encontrar soluciones sencillas y potentes, con una estética atrevida y un resultado sorprendente en las diversas plataformas. Su trabajo se ha descrito de alegre pero serio, equilibrio que se esfuerzan por conservar.

It's Nice That escribe que su trabajo es «abstracto hasta el nivel adecuado y con una gama de colores fuera de lo normal», mientras que la revista AIGA les denomina «El estudio de diseño gráfico más amable de toda Italia».

Busk Poster (left page)

Busk, by Studio Mut

Busk, by Studio Mut

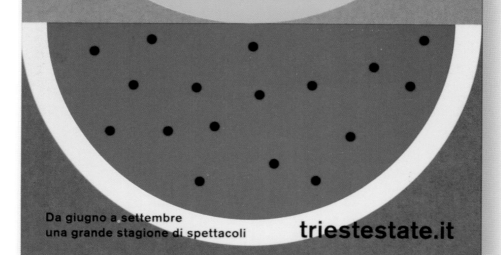

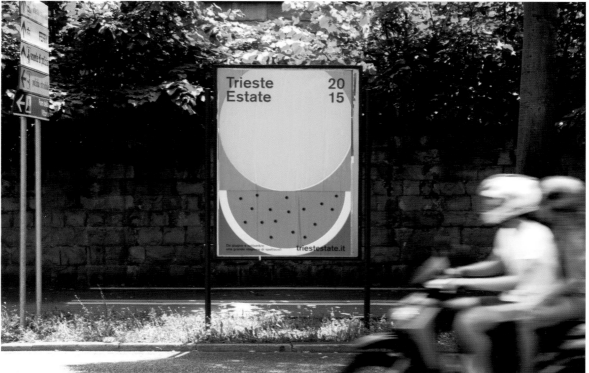

Trieste Estate, by Studio Mut

Trieste Estate

20 16

Promossa e organizzata da

comune di trieste

con il contributo di

UniCredit

EstEnergy

Da giugno a settembre
una grande stagione di spettacoli

triestestate.it

Trieste Estate, by Studio Mut

BRIGHTON64
DV25NOV
PASTERNAK

Quim Marin

www.quimmarin.com

Looking back on to Quim Marin work one can realize that it is strongly linked to the show business. Particularly to music. Quim finds it hard to count the projects he has worked in throughout the last 15 years. Naming, art direction, graphic design, creation of advertising campaigns – "I believe I have pulled all the strings".

He thanks the music scene for its extreme sensitiveness to the passing of time and trends. Working in it has forged in him a plastic spirit; it has forced him to be under a constant creative evolution. In this sphere there is a vast offer and its public are avid and fleeting –but often fickle– consumers. "To stand out is essential, and creativity is the means to achieve it. To my mind, however, not everything goes. I have my own recipe. In such a visually polluted environment I try to come up with fresh and memorable designs with a clear aim at essential beauty and equilibrium that, at the same time, will ensure communicative effectiveness. I seek to whet the eye, I want the visual impact to remain in people's memory, I aspire to seduce minds through contrast".

Si nos fijamos en la obra de Quim Marin nos daremos cuenta de que está muy vinculada con el mundo del espectáculo. Principalmente el de la música. Quim es incapaz de enumerar los proyectos en los que ha trabajado en los últimos 15 años. Denominación, dirección artística, diseño gráfico, creación de campañas publicitarias – "Creo que he tocado todos los palos".

Agradece al sector musical su extrema sensibilidad al paso del tiempo y las tendencias. Trabajar en este mundo ha forjado en él un espíritu plástico, le ha obligado a estar en constante evolución creativa. En esta ámbito existe una inmensa oferta y el público está formado por consumidores ansiosos y fugaces, aunque a menudo variables. "Destacar es fundamental, y la creatividad es la forma de conseguirlo. No obstante, en mi mente no todo vale. Tengo mi propia receta. En un entorno tan contaminado a nivel visual, intento ofrecer diseños frescos y memorables con un objetivo claro de belleza esencial y equilibrio que, al mismo tiempo, garanticen una eficacia comunicativa. Busco tentar a la vista, quiero que el impacto visual permanezca en la memoria del espectador, aspiro a seducir la mente mediante el contraste."

Brighton (left page)

Masimas festival poster, by Quim Marin

Dv15Gener
Johnny Quid —*Dj*
—
Sala
Pasternak
Vic

Dissabte 7 Maig
Pasternak
Vic

Dj Johnny
Quid

salapasternak
.com

Entrada gratuïta

Divendres 22
Gener 2016
—
Sala Pasternak
Vic
—
Dj Capo

salapasternak.com
entrada gratuïta

DS—08
MANIAC MARC
DJ—

24.OOH
Sala Pasternak—Vic
—Entrada gratuïta

Indie
Rock, Pop
&Electrònica

www.
salapasternak
.com

DS
08'06
2013

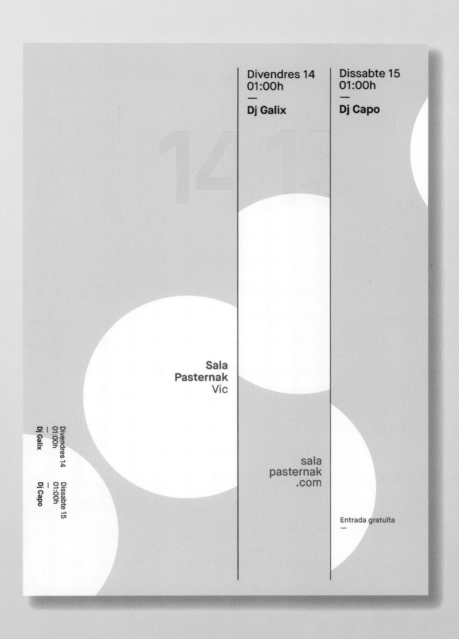

Posters, by Quim Marin

17.05.13
23H
GRATUÏT

Maniac
Marc
—Dj.

PASTER
NAK

Posters, by Quim Marin

WINTER 2011

KALEID

MICHELLE
WILLIAMS

PHOTOGRAPHY:
MIKAEL JANSSON

A BIG BREATH
Florence and
The Machine

CAN WE WEATHER
THE STORM?
David Johnston

ESSAY:
The man who built
his own house

UK £7

Aidan Stonehouse

cargocollective.com/aidanstonehouse

Aidan Stonehouse is a Graphic Designer based in Manchester England. Having spent several years working as a Designer for Creative Agencies in London, Aidan went on to become a Freelance Designer working across branding and digital before heading back to Manchester to work full-time in a Digital Agency. Aidan has worked with clients such Sony, Sainsburys and Just Eat and designed for projects that have been displayed around the globe, Kaleid however is still one of his favourite projects.

Aidan Stonehouse es un diseñador gráfico establecido en Manchester, Inglaterra. Tras trabajar varios años como diseñador para agencias creativas en Londres, Aidan pasó a trabajar como diseñador independiente especializado en branding y medios digitales, antes de regresar a Manchester para desempeñar sus funciones a jornada completa en una agencia digital. Aidan ha trabajado para clientes como Sony, Sainsburys y Just Eat y participado en proyectos de diseño presentes con alcance mundial, aunque el de Kaleid sigue siendo uno de sus favoritos.

CONTENTS

ARTS

FILM

MUSIC

CULTURE

Photography Mikael Jansson
Stylist Karl Templer

> One of the best things—and something I'm grateful for every time I walk onto a film set—is my six and a half years on Dawson's Creek and the experience it afforded me in how to get comfortable with the camera. The best acting classes I ever took.

MICHELLE WILLIAMS

VENDELA VIDA: I know you were born in Montana, but are you of Scandinavian descent?

MICHELLE WILLIAMS: I'm Norwegian.

VIDA: I thought so, because *Ingrid* is your middle name and your mom has a Scandinavian-sounding maiden name: Swenson. Did you ever hear Norwegian in the household, or did you ever go back to Norway?

WILLIAMS: No, I've never been, and my mom didn't speak it. We made a lot of *lefse*, a Norwegian dessert, to compensate. I was talking to my grandma on the phone maybe a month ago, and she said, 'Did you ever hear this story about Inge Jacobs?' I said, 'No, but it's a great name, Inge Jacobs. Tell me about Inge Jacobs.' Inge Jacobs would be my great, great grandmother, I think, and she was a stowaway. At 15 years old, she got on a boat from Norway, made it to Ellis Island, and then hopped on a covered wagon, and that's how they got to Montana. I loved that one after I made Meek's.

VIDA: That's so weird. Traveling in a covered wagon is in your blood.

WILLIAMS: Yes, some part of me has done this journey before.

VIDA: And didn't you go off and live on your own when you were 15, too?

WILLIAMS: I did. It gave me so much comfort. Why did I have that urge? I think it was Inge Jacobs's bones kicking around in me.

VIDA: When you went to live on your own, did you go to L.A.?

WILLIAMS: Yeah. I went to L.A. At that point my family was living in San Diego, so it wasn't as big an undertaking as Inge Jacobs's. I hopped around from crappy apartment complex to crappy apartment complex in the Los Angeles area.

VIDA: Were you still close to your family? Or was it one of those breaks you make when you're 15 and later patch things up?

WILLIAMS: It was kind of a break. It didn't last too terribly long, thank goodness, before I got Dawson's Creek and moved to North Carolina.

VIDA: Do you remember anything about getting your first apartment? I ask because when I was 19, I somehow convinced my parents to let me go dormsitting by myself

and I remember checking into an inexpensive hotel in Paris. First thing I did was buy a baguette and some YOP drinkable yogurt and place them on a windowsill with a view of Paris in the background. I took a picture of that image—to me, that photo symbolized freedom.

WILLIAMS: I had always been kind of obsessed with making a home of my own and was always dreaming rooms that I wanted to live in, down to pictures on the wall and the faces that would be in the photographs, and how the swatches would be situated. I just remember missing furniture around a lot. I remember that the first included with the Ikea furniture promised to assemble everything but didn't. It was all right somewhat, by the way, Norwegian looking, the sales guy told me. I sat in frustration with a lot of cardboard boxes around me, eating Clif bars for dinner because I couldn't cook. I was making house, but at night, because no one was there telling me to go to bed, I still have a hard time giving up on the day and admitting exhaustion.

VIDA: Let's talk a little bit about Meek's Cutoff, which is the second film you've done with director Kelly Reichardt—the first being Wendy and Lucy. I was wondering what it was like to work on more than one film with the same director. Do you feel because you've spent so much time together at this point that you have kind of a shorthand when working together?

WILLIAMS: You know the safety you feel when a man asks you to marry him?

VIDA: Mm-hmm....

WILLIAMS: It felt like she doesn't just want to date me. She wants to marry me.

VIDA: Did you know from the beginning that you'd be doing two films with her?

WILLIAMS: No, I feel no idea. One day she came over to our house in Brooklyn with a manila envelope, and said she had something special to give me. So we walked upstairs and sat on my bed, and she handed me the first draft of Meek's. It really is one of the top five favorite moments of my life—it's right up there. Because I wasn't expecting it. And I married it. I hope to make movies with her for a long time to come. So I guess at this point, knowing Kelly has been like an education on film. Not that she's ever tried to teach me, but just sort of by osmosis, and being her friend, and understanding what she likes, and having her reference movies, and then going and

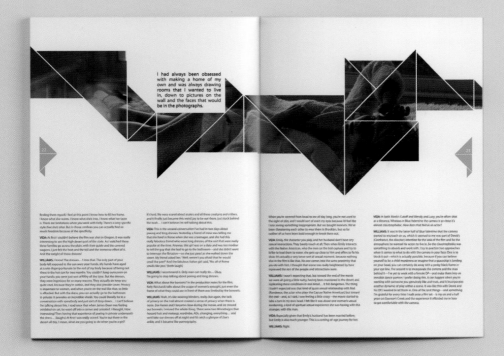

> I had always been obsessed with making a home of my own and was always drawing rooms that I wanted to live in, down to pictures on the wall and the faces that would be in the photographs.

Project Name:
Kaleid - Arts & Cultures Magazine

Client: Kaleid Magazine

Arts & Culture has so many facets and it's the idea of all these shapes, styles and colours that were the inspiration behind the name and style of 'Kaleid' magazine. From this initial seed a brand was developed that went on to inform a unique visual style which continued throughout the magazine.

Arts & Culture tiene muchas facetas y refleja la idea de todas las formas, estilos y colores que han inspirado el nombre y estilo de la revista 'Kaleid'. Desde sus inicios, se desarrolló una marca que conformase un estilo visual único presente de manera continuada en la revista.

Editorial design

Seraina Lareida

www.serainalareida.ch
www.portego.it

Seraina Lareida is a young Swiss designer currently based in Bern/Switzerland. After one year living and working in London, she returned to Switzerland in order to accomplish her MA in Product Design at the ECAL in Lausanne. Ever since, she has been exhibiting her work at renowned places like Design Miami Basel, Bikini Berlin, Maison&Objet Paris, ISPO Munich, Salone Internazionale del Mobile Milan and Musée de Design et d'Arts Appliqués Contemporains Lausanne. Currently, she is working as product designer at USM Möbelbausysteme, Swiss leader for interior and office furniture. She is also initiating own projects in collaboration with local manufacturers, design labels and art galleries.

Seraina Lareida es una joven diseñadora suiza que actualmente reside en Berna, Suiza. Tras un año viviendo y trabajando en Londres, volvió a Suiza para realizar su Máster en Diseño de Productos en la ECAL de Lausana. Desde entonces, ha expuesto su trabajo en lugares de renombre como Design Miami Basel, Bikini Berlin, Maison&Objet Paris, ISPO Munich, el Salone Internazionale del Mobile de Milán y el Musée de Design et d'Arts Appliqués Contemporains de Lausana. En la actualidad trabaja como diseñadora de productos en USM Möbelbausysteme, líder suiza de interiorismo y mobiliario de oficinas. Además, lleva a cabo proyectos propios en colaboración con fabricantes locales, agencias de diseño y galerías de arte.

Portego's rug collection (left page)

Sottoportico rug, by Seraina Lareida

Sottovolto rug, by Seraina Lareida

Project Name: Sottoportico / Sottovolto

Client: Portego

The designs are inspired by forms and shapes of venetian architecture through the centuries. They playfully interact with the surrounding water in a spray of colours and reflections.

Los diseños se inspiran en las formas utilizadas durante siglos en la arquitectura veneciana. Estas interactúan de manera alegre con el agua que las rodea, en un rocío de colores y reflejos.

Product Design

Jae Won Cho

www.j1studio.com

Born in South Korea, Jae Won Cho graduated in Environmental Design at the Art Center College of Design in Pasadena, California. In 2008 he founded J1 Studio, a furniture design studio located in Los Angeles, California. His work has been featured in numerous international publications including Fast Company, Ready Made, Architecture Digest Spain and Vogue. He was also recently featured in Design and Architecture, hosted by Frances Anderton on KCRW.

Recent exhibitions include the Architecture and Design Museum, Design Matters gallery and M.A.D.E (Los Angeles). Jae Won Cho lives and works between Los Angeles and Seoul.

Nacido en Corea del Sur, Jae Won Cho se graduó en Diseño Medioambiental en el Art Center College of Design de Pasadena, California. En 2008 fundó J1 Studio, un estudio de diseño de mobiliario situado en Los Ángeles, California. Su trabajo ha aparecido en numerosas publicaciones internacionales, entre ellas Fast Company, Ready Made, Architecture Digest España y Vogue. Además, recientemente se ha incluido en Design and Architecture, de Frances Anderton, en KCRW.

Entre sus últimas exposiciones encontramos las realizadas en el Architecture and Design Museum, la Design Matters Gallery y el M.A.D.E (Los Ángeles). Jae Won Cho vive y trabaja entre Los Ángeles y Seúl.

The C.lamp (left page)

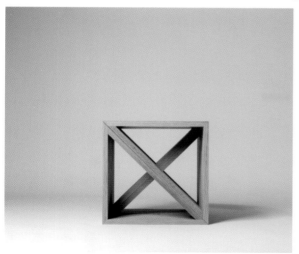
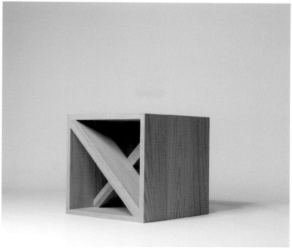

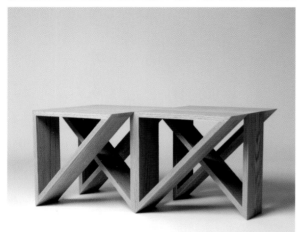

Project Name: The M.STOOL

Seating arrangement composed of three triangular forms.
Developed as a sculptural play block, the modular design
can be arranged to various shapes.
Two M.stools build a cube. Eight M.stools can form a circle.

Asiento compuesto por tres formas triangulares.
Desarrollado como bloque de juego escultural, el diseño
modular se puede organizar de varias formas.
Dos M.stools componen un cubo. Ocho M.stools pueden
formar un círculo.

Furniture design

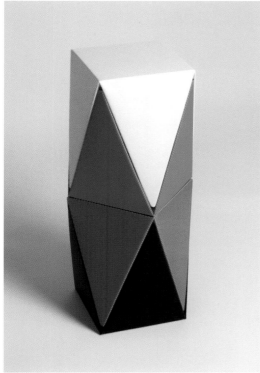

Project Name: The V.STAND

Named after the triangle (V) shaped leg, V.STAND is a multi-purpose side table that holds small objects such as plants, books, clock, phone, speakers etc. It features a sturdy and stable design that can be used indoors and outdoors as a side table, adding a colorful accent with a friendly character to the environment. Constructed with corrugated plastic using a folding technique, it weights less than one pound and can hold up to 75lbs without damaging the tips of the legs. When V.STANDS are not in use, it can stack vertically to save space.

Conocido por la "de las patas en forma de triángulo (V)", la V.stand es una mesa multiusos ideal para pequeños objetos como plantas, libros, relojes, altavoces, etc. Su diseño es robusto y estable, y puede utilizarse tanto en interiores como en exteriores como mesa auxiliar, añadiendo un toque de color con carácter alegre al ambiente.
Fabricada en plástico corrugado utilizando una técnica de plegado, pesa menos de 500 gramos y soporta hasta 34 kilogramos sin que los extremos de las patas resulten dañados. Cuando las V.stand no se utilizan, se puede apilar en vertical para ahorrar espacio.

Furniture design

II Festival de Filosofia
Del 16 al 21 de Novembre de 2015

Barcelona
Pensa

#BCNPensa
www.barcelonapensa.cat

Studio Carreras

www.studiocarreras.com
instagram: studiocarreras

Studio Carreras is the independent design studio of Genís Carreras, a graphic designer, illustrator and author based in Girona, Spain. Specialised in brand identity, art direction, print, icon design and editorial for clients both big and small from all around the globe. Carreras uses colour and simple shapes to create ingenious, minimal and unique pieces of visual communication for brands, events and publications.

Studio Carreras es el estudio de diseño independiente de Genís Carreras, diseñador gráfico, ilustrador y autor ubicado en Girona, España. El estudio está especializado en identidad de marca, dirección artística, impresión, diseño de iconos y diseño editorial para clientes tanto grandes como pequeños de todo el mundo. Carreras utiliza el color y las formas simples para crear piezas únicas, ingeniosas y minimalistas de comunicación visual para marcas, eventos y publicaciones.

Barcelona Pensa 2015 (left page)

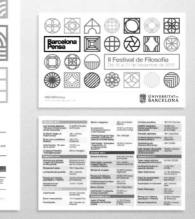

Barcelona Pensa 2015, by Studio Carreras

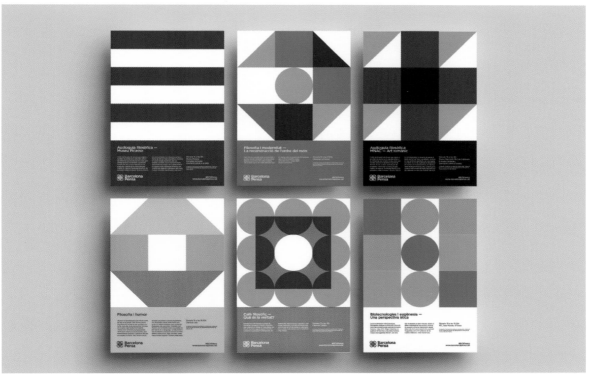

Barcelona Pensa 2016, by Studio Carreras

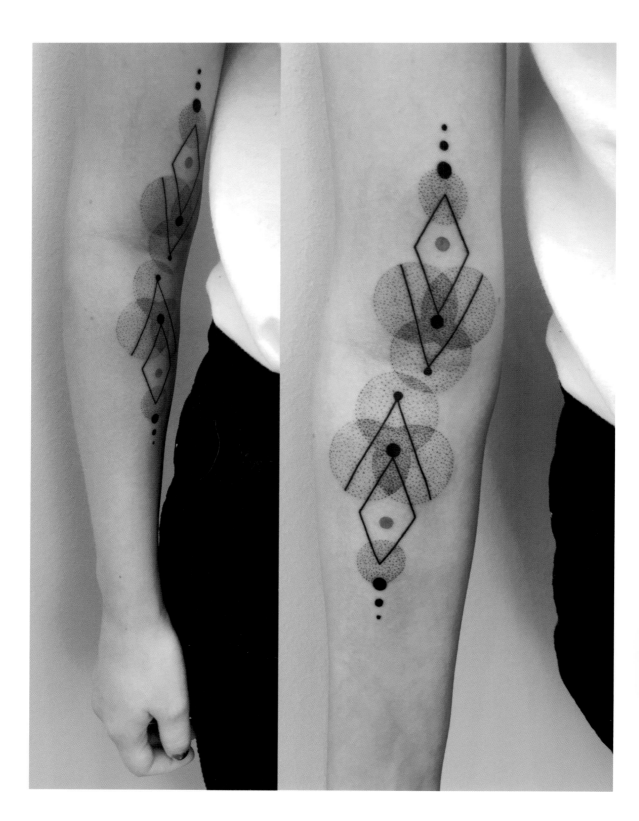

Marta Slawinska

www.axelejsmont.com
instagram: axelejsmont

The work of Polish visual artist Marta Slawinska, born 1981 in Warsaw, is situated in abstract geometrical tribal ornament. Her interest goes in relationship between primitive and contemporary art. The artist, who studied at Warsaw Academy of Fine Arts and L'ecole Estienne now is based in Berlin. Since ten years established position as a illustrator working for Die Zeit, Weltkunst, The mail and Globe, the Sunday times, Wrap magazine and many more. In 2014 Marta published in Germany her children book "Der kleine Nasenbohrer". Four years ago she established her position as a tattoo artist. Her interested goes in video projections and instalations.

La obra de la artista visual polaca Marta Slawinska, nacida en 1981 en Varsovia, se puede calificar de ornamentación tribal geométrica abstracta. Sus intereses guardan relación con el arte tanto primitivo como contemporáneo. Esta artista, que estudió en la Academia de Bellas Artes de Varsovia y L'ecole Estienne, vive actualmente en Berlín. Tras diez años como ilustradora reconocida, ha trabajado para Die Zeit, Weltkunst, The Globe and Mail, The Sunday Times, Wrap Magazine y muchos otros clientes. En 2014, Marta publicó su libro infantil "Der kleine Nasenbohrer" en Alemania. Hace cuatro años, se estableció como artista tatuadora. Está interesada en proyecciones de vídeo e instalaciones.

Untilted Axel Ejsmont's Tattoo (left page)

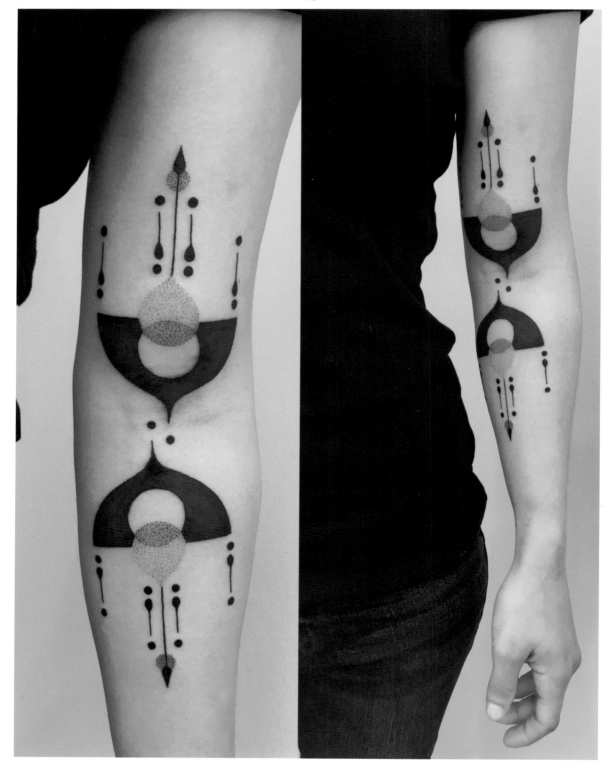

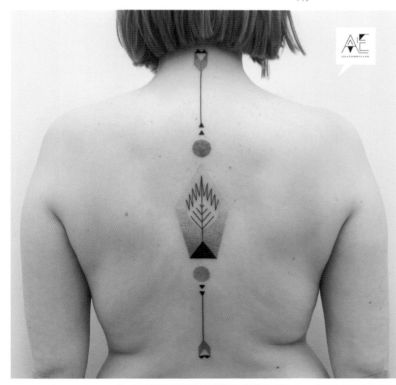

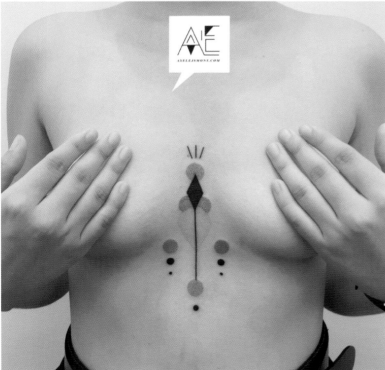

Project Name: Axel Ejsmont

Client: Various

Axel Ejsmont its a tattoo project wich is ongoing since 2013. Marta Slawinska work is a summary of an art practice and past experience as a graphic designer and illustrator. Her tattoos oscillate between visual minimalism and graphic geometrical ornaments. The designs in Axel Ejsmont work are often built on combinations of repeated triangels and circles, which may be overlapped and intelaced to form intricate and complex patterns.

Axel Ejsmont es un proyecto de tatuaje iniciado en 2013. La obra de Marta Slawinska es un resumen de práctica artística y experiencia pasada como diseñadora gráfica e ilustradora. Sus tatuajes oscilan entre el minimalismo visual y los ornamentos geométricos gráficos. Los diseños de la obra Axel Ejsmont a menudo están formados por combinaciones de triángulos y círculos repetidos, que se pueden superponer y entrelazar formando patrones intrincados y complejos.

Tattoo design

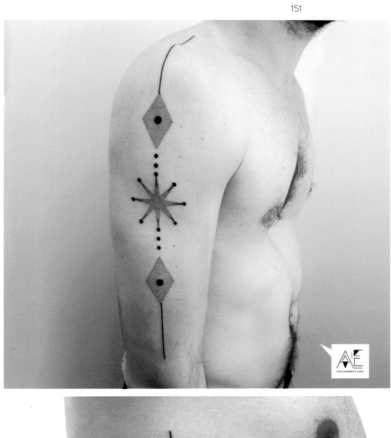

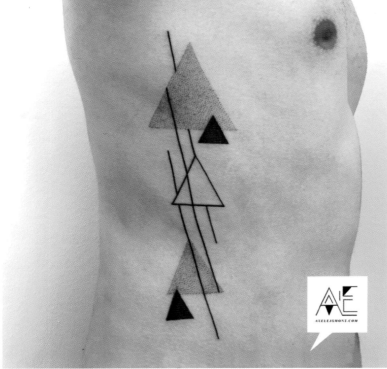

Axel Ejsmont's Tattoo by Marta Slawinska

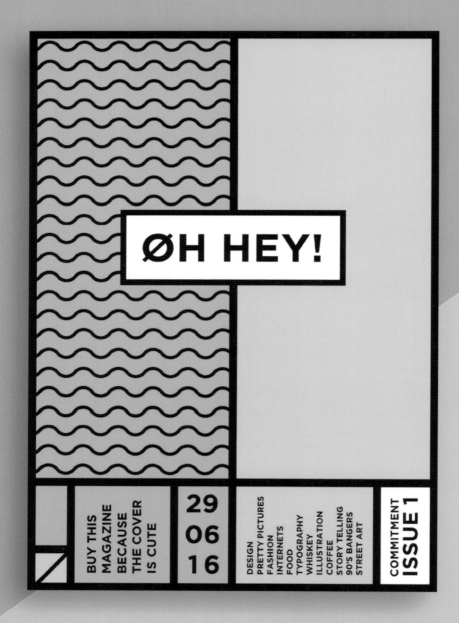

Shanti Sparrow

www.shantisparrow.com

Shanti Sparrow is an Australian graphic designer, illustrator, lecturer and dreamer. She has been freelancing internationally and working within boutique studios for the last decade. Sparrow has specialised as a conceptual designer focusing on fundraising and awareness campaigns. Sparrow is known as the queen of layout and her work is characteristically informed by the grid with refined typography and bold color choices. As an illustrator Sparrow has created a unique style involving scanned textures, vector patterns and digital collage. These dreamlike scenes engage the child in us all with their playful and enchanting aesthetic. Sparrow has published four children's picture books though Hardie Grant and Pomegranate Publishing.

Shanti Sparrow es una diseñadora gráfica, ilustradora, profesora y soñadora australiana. Ha trabajado de manera independiente a nivel internacional y colaborado con estudios boutique durante la última década. Sparrow se ha especializado en el diseño conceptual, centrándose en campañas de concienciación y recaudación de fondos. Es conocida como la "reina del diseño" y su obra se caracteriza por su refinada tipografía y llamativas elecciones de color. Como ilustradora, Sparrow ha creado un estilo único que incorpora texturas escaneadas, patrones de vectores y collages digitales. Estas escenas de ensueño cautivan al niño que llevamos dentro gracias a su alegre y hechizante estética. Sparrow ha publicado cuatro libros de imágenes infantiles a través de Hardie Grant y Pomegranate Publishing.

Oh Hey! magazine (left page)

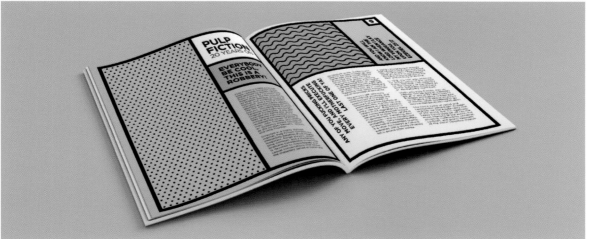

Oh Hey! magazine by Shanti Sparrow

Antonia Skaraki

www.antoniaskaraki.com

Since the early '90s, Antonia Skaraki worked as head of the art department for several newspapers and magazines and served as a creative director for Able Communications advertising. During 1993, she founded Karamella, one of the top advertising agencies, while participating actively against racial segregation in workplace environments. In 2007, Antonia became partner of Looking advertising company and today, she runs a smaller but rather successful design and branding company consisted of trustworthy graphic designers and communication experts. Their doctrine is based in today's multipurpose demands of the market and client oriented drives.

Desde principios de los 90, Antonia Skaraki ha trabajado como directora del departamento artístico de diversos periódicos y revistas, y desempeñado funciones como directora creativa de la publicidad de Able Communications. En 1993, fundó Karamella, agencia de publicidad de primer nivel, mientras participaba de manera activa contra la segregación racial en el lugar de trabajo. En 2007, Antonia pasó a asociarse con la compañía de publicidad Looking y en la actualidad dirige una pequeña pero exitosa empresa de diseño y branding en la que trabajan diseñadores y expertos en comunicación de confianza. Su doctrina se basa en la demanda multiusos actual del mercado y las iniciativas orientadas al cliente.

IONIA Limited Edition (left page)

Project Name: IONIA Limited Edition

Client: Nutria

Each bottle is individually designed. It is a one-of-a-kind linear design, inspired from ancient Greek patterns with a modern touch that celebrates a vintage olive oil heritage. The greyish-brown colors highlight the roots of this premium quality extra virgin olive oil.

Cada botella se diseña de manera individual. Se trata de un diseño lineal exclusivo, inspirado en antiguos patrones griegos con un toque moderno que celebra la herencia clásica asociada al aceite de oliva. Sus tonos marrones grisáceos resaltan las raíces de este aceite de oliva virgen extra de calidad premium.

Packaging design

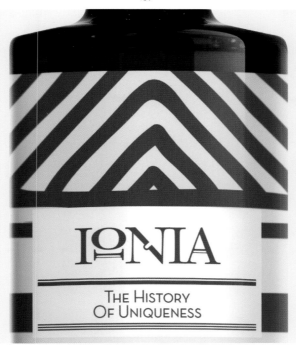

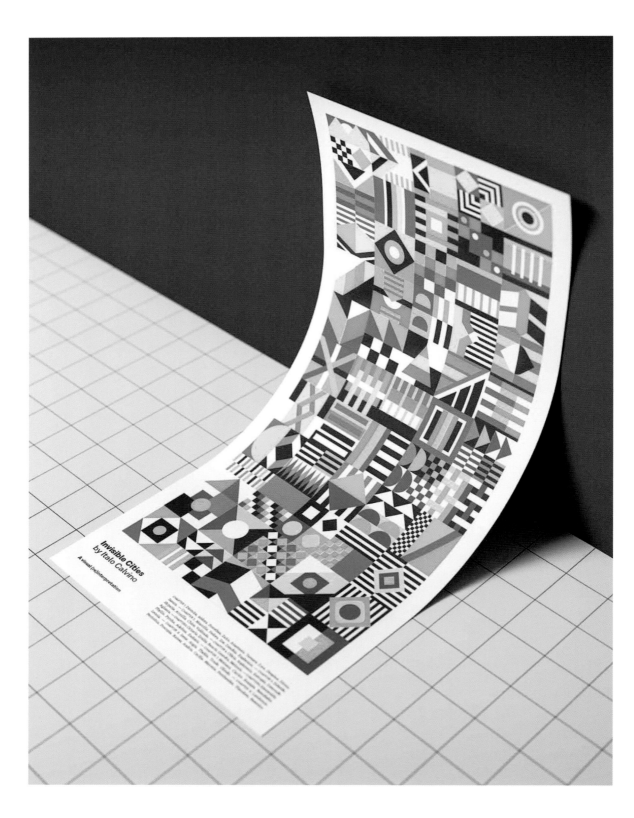

Invisible Cities
by Italo Calvino

A visual (re)interpretation

Serafim Mendes

www.serafimmendes.com
www.behance.net/serafimmendes

Serafim Mendes is a graphic designer based in Porto, Portugal. His main areas of interest are typography, editorial design and 3D illustration. He has a particular passion for geometric work, with simple yet strong visuals.

Serafim Mendes es un diseñador gráfico residente en Oporto, Portugal. Sus principales campos de interés son la tipografía, el diseño editorial y la ilustración en 3D. Tiene una pasión particular por las obras geométricas, con elementos visuales sencillos pero contundentes.

Invisible Cities poster (left page)

Invisible Cities
by Italo Calvino

A visual (re)interpretation

Project Name: Invisible Cities

Invisible Cities is his visual interpretation of the book Invisible Cities by Italo Calvino, first published in 1972. It aims to present its content in a different form, through a visual representation of the original text. As such, each one of the cities was illustrated through a geometrical representation, providing the reader with a different kind of interpretation, without limiting his imagination, but rather stimulating it.

Invisible Cities es su interpretación visual del libro Invisible Cities de Italo Calvino, publicado inicialmente en 1972. Pretende presentar su contenido de un modo distinto, a través de una representación visual del texto original. Así, cada una de las ciudades se ha ilustrado mediante una representación geométrica, permitiendo al lector realizar un tipo de interpretación diferente, sin poner límites a su imaginación, pero estimulando la misma.

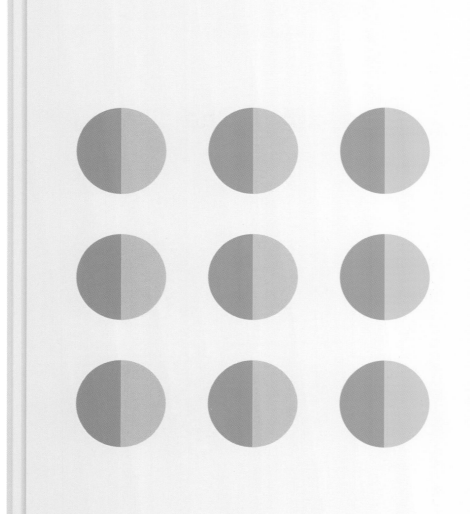

Minji Cha

www.behance.net/chaminji

Minji Cha is a graphic designer based in Seoul, Korea.

He wrote a manifesto and created a project when he just started studying graphic design and he still do believe these statements stand for him beliefs and strategies in design.

Minji Cha es un diseñador gráfico residente en Seúl, Corea.

Nada más empezar a estudiar diseño gráfico redactó un manifiesto y creó un proyecto, cuyas declaraciones siguen siendo la base de sus creencias y estrategias en materia de diseño.

Good Design Manifesto (left page)

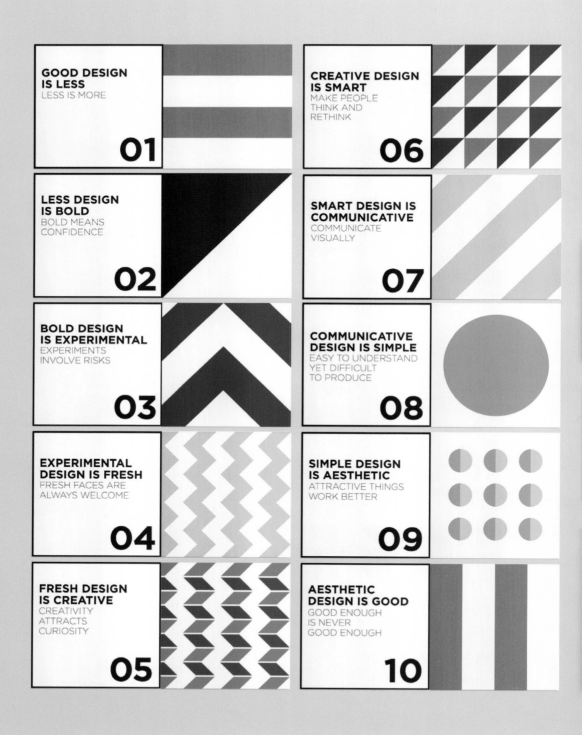

GOOD DESIGN IS LESS
LESS IS MORE
01

LESS DESIGN IS BOLD
BOLD MEANS CONFIDENCE
02

BOLD DESIGN IS EXPERIMENTAL
EXPERIMENTS INVOLVE RISKS
03

EXPERIMENTAL DESIGN IS FRESH
FRESH FACES ARE ALWAYS WELCOME
04

FRESH DESIGN IS CREATIVE
CREATIVITY ATTRACTS CURIOSITY
05

CREATIVE DESIGN IS SMART
MAKE PEOPLE THINK AND RETHINK
06

SMART DESIGN IS COMMUNICATIVE
COMMUNICATE VISUALLY
07

COMMUNICATIVE DESIGN IS SIMPLE
EASY TO UNDERSTAND YET DIFFICULT TO PRODUCE
08

SIMPLE DESIGN IS AESTHETIC
ATTRACTIVE THINGS WORK BETTER
09

AESTHETIC DESIGN IS GOOD
GOOD ENOUGH IS NEVER GOOD ENOUGH
10

BOLD DESIGN
IS EXPERIMEN
EXPERIMENTS
INVOLVE RISKS

SIMPLE DESIGN

FRESH DESIGN

**GOOD DESIGN
IS LESS**
LESS IS MORE

01

Project Name: Good Design Manifesto

Client: Self publication

Design

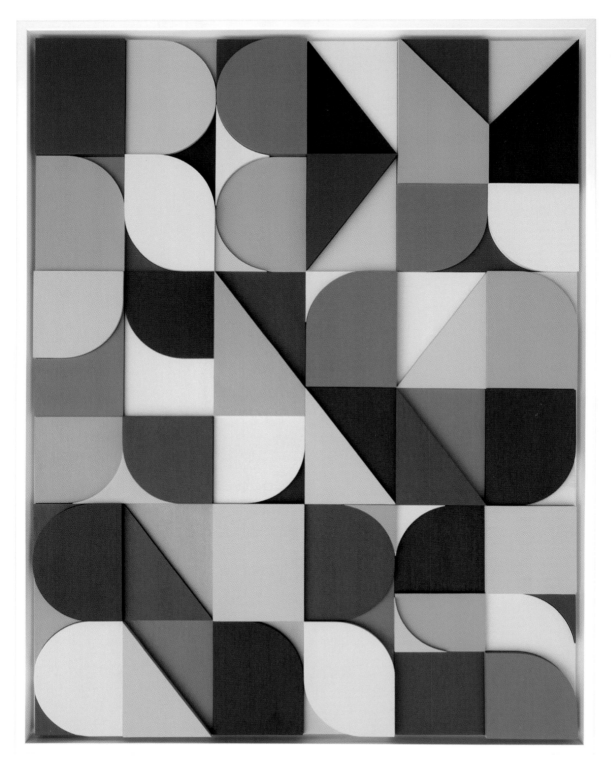

Scott Albrecht

ScottAlbrecht.com

Currently based in Brooklyn, NY, Scott Albrecht's work is made from a shared interest of art and design, often acting as a distillation of his daily experiences into a his own brand of graphic abstractions.

La obra de Scott Albrechtm que actualmente tiene su residencia en Brooklyn, NY, se basa en un interés compartido en el arte y el diseño, que a menudo actúa como síntesis de sus experiencias cotidianas en sus abstracciones gráficas de marca propia.

Reminders (left page)

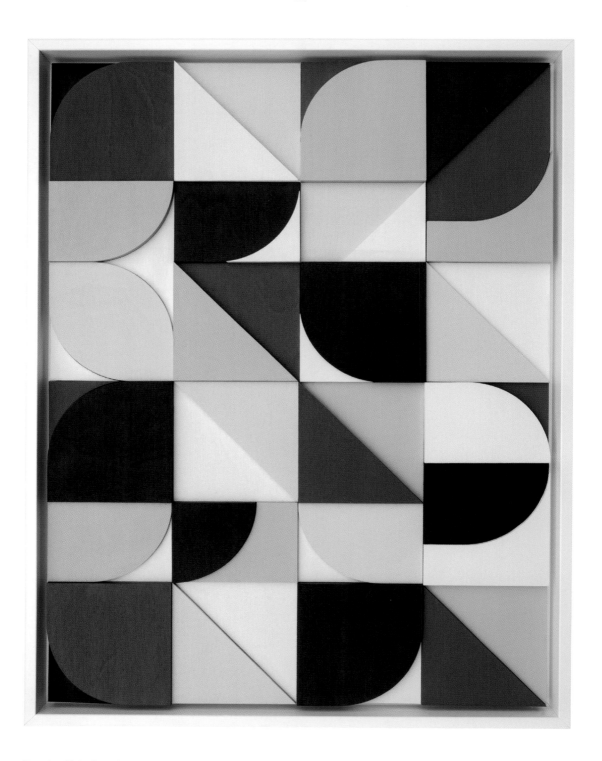

Hear / ereH, by Scott Albrecht

Then & Now, by Scott Albrecht

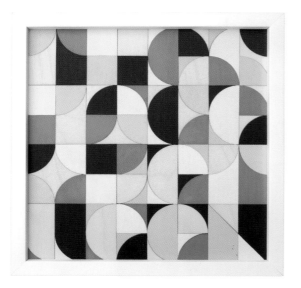

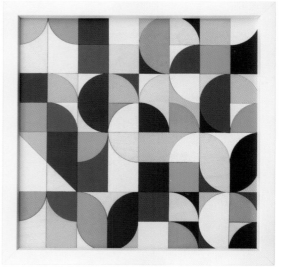

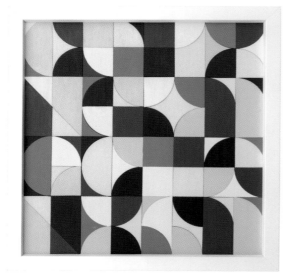

The Space Between and **The Present Future** (on top),
Coping Mechanism, by Scott Albrecht

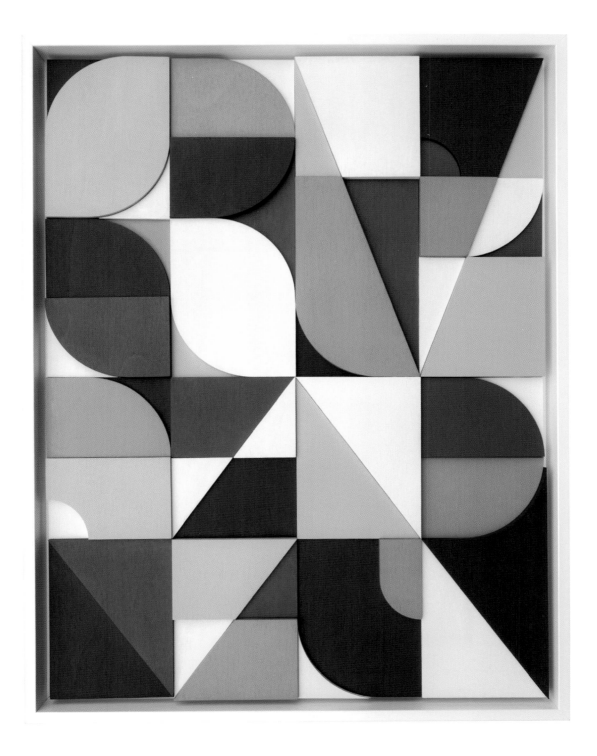

Over / revO, by Scott Albrecht

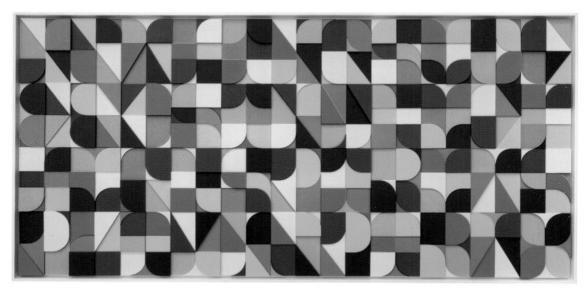

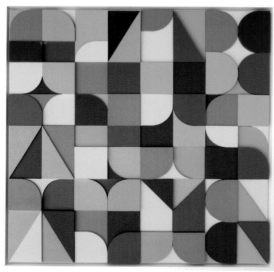

Nothing Succeeds in Which High Spirits Play No Part (on top), **All This Time** and **The Present,** by Scott Albrecht

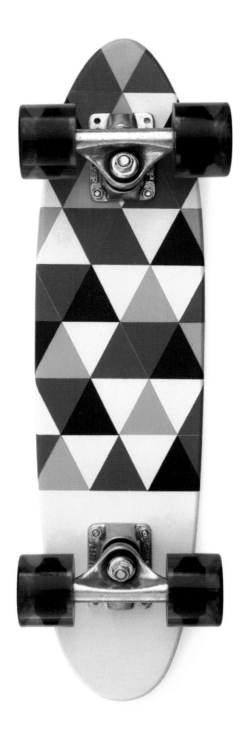 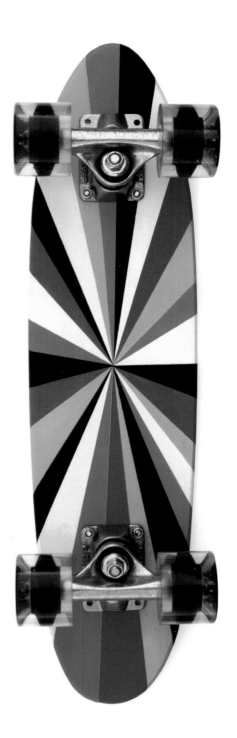

Cruiser No. 3 and **Cruiser No. 4,** by Scott Albrecht

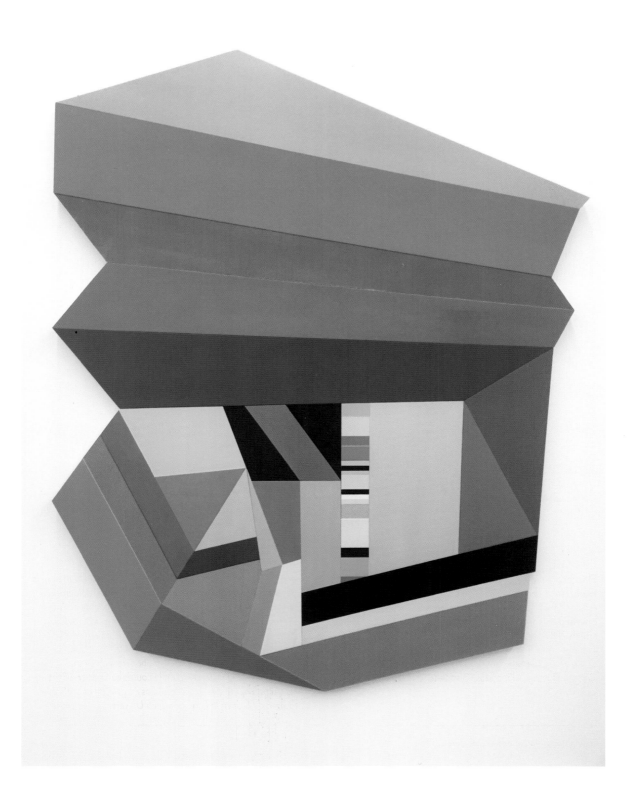

Joey Slaughter

www.joeyslaughter.com

Slaughter earned his BFA from Memphis College of Art in 1997. He received his MFA from Cranbrook Academy of Art in 2000. Upon graduating Cranbrook, Slaughter was awarded the prestigious Joan Mitchell Foundation Grant and in 2006 and was nominated for the Louis Comfort Tiffany Grant. In 2012 he received the Louisiana Division of the Arts, Career Enhancement Grant. He is currently living in Ruston, LA, and is Associate Professor of Art at Louisiana Tech University.

Slaughter obtuvo su Licenciatura en Bellas Artes en la Memphis College of Art en 1997. Más tarde, en el año 2000, lograría su Máster en Bellas Artes en la Cranbrook Academy of Art. Tras graduarse en Cranbrook, Slaughter consiguió una de las prestigiosas becas de la Joan Mitchell Foundation y en 2006 fue nominado para hacerse con una beca de Louis Comfort Tiffany. En 2012 recibió la Career Enhancement Grant (Beca a la Mejora Formativa) de la Louisiana Division of the Arts. Actualmente vive en Ruston, Los Ángeles, y es profesor asociado de arte en la Louisiana Tech University.

Telling things you already know (left page)

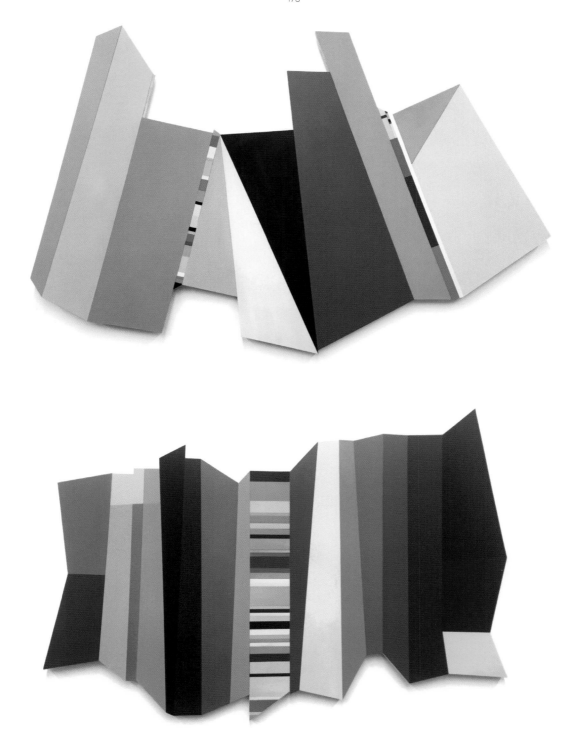

10,000 hours and no accolades (on top), **Loose lips sinks ships** (bottom), by Joey Slaughter

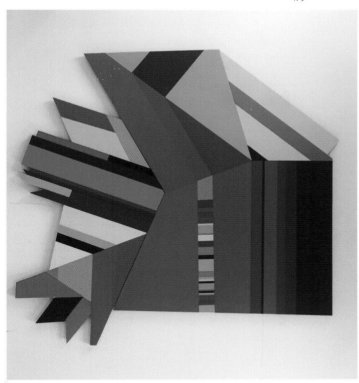

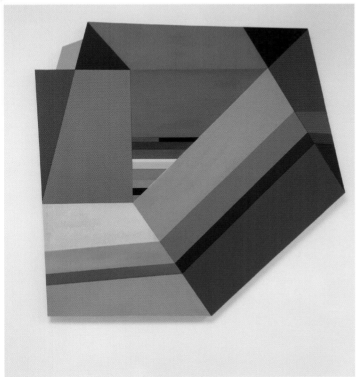

The bad bad, not good (on top), **That's where the goods are** (bottom), by Joey Slaughter

Simek

www.behance.net/simek

Christos Tzaferos is Simek a visual artist.

Born in 1985 in Greece. Has been experimenting with graffiti & street art since the beginning of 2000.

Studied Graphic Design in Athens. Took up painting and photography in 2009 while working as a visual artist. He work with design, murals, papers, collage, installation among other things. From 2011 until now he is collaborating with the artist Greg Papagrigoriou under the name "Blaqk".

Christos Tzaferos es el artista visual Simek.

Nació en 1985 en Grecia. Desde el año 2000 ha experimentado con el grafiti y el arte callejero.

Estudió diseño gráfico en Atenas. En 2009 comenzó a dedicarse a la pintura y la fotografía mientras trabajaba como artista visual. Realiza trabajos de diseño y obras en mural, papel, collages, instalaciones, etc. Desde 2011 hasta la actualidad ha colaborado con el artista Greg Papagrigoriou bajo el nombre de "Blaqk".

Athens, Greece by Simek & Seikon (left page)

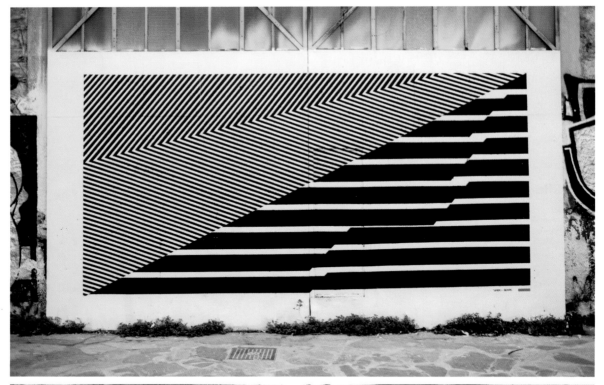

Athens, Greece by Simek & Seikon / photo: Alka Murat - **Black Circle Festival, Ukraine** by Simek & Seikon

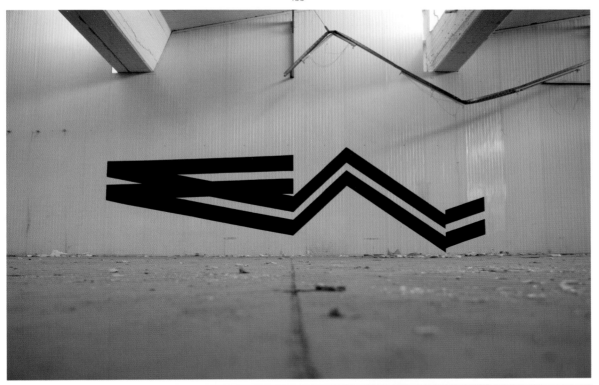

Chalkida, Greece by Simek / photo: Dimitris Vasiliou

Chalkida, Greece by Simek / photo: Dimitris Vasiliou - **Black Circle Festival, Ukraine** by Simek

Giclee print on fine art paper 35x50cm, by Simek

Setup

www.setuptype.com

Setup is a Slovak type foundry and graphic design studio founded in 2009 by Ondrej Jób. The studio's activities range from designing retail and custom typefaces, to lettering, corporate identity, editorial design or icon and pictogram design for both print and screen.

The studio is run by Ondrej Jób, a type and graphic designer currently living in Bratislava, Slovakia. He holds MA degree in graphic design from Academy of Fine Arts and Design in Bratislava, Slovakia (2008) and in type design from TypeMedia masters program at The Royal Academy of Arts (KABK) in Den Haag, the Netherlands (2009).

Setup es un estudio de diseño gráfico y tipos eslovaca fundada en 2009 por Ondrej Jób. Entre las actividades del estudio encontramos desde el diseño de tipografías personalizadas y al por menor hasta el diseño de rótulos, identidades corporativas, diseño editorial o diseño de iconos y pictogramas tanto para medios impresos como digitales.

Ondrej Jób, diseñador gráfico y tipográfico que actualmente reside en Bratislava, Eslovaquia, dirige el estudio. Ondrej cuenta con un Máster en Diseño Gráfico de la Academia de Bellas Artes y Diseño de Bratislava, Eslovaquia (2008) y otro en Diseño de Tipografías y Medios de la Real Academia de Artes (KABK) de Den Haag, Holanda (2009).

Pecha Kucha Night Bratislava Vol. 25 Poster (left page)

Early Melons 2011 Masterclass Poster by Setup

Early Melons 2011 Videofizz Poster by Setup